MW00572167

Deidre B. Hester
Sue E. Whited

To:
Claudia

Keep touching the future. You are one of God's tools and a mouthpiece. I love you,

Deidre B. Hester
Voice # I

"Teacher to Teacher"
You are blessed - Keep up
the great work you're doing in
your area.

Claudia,
Such a pleasure
to meet you and share
our "voices." May
you be blessed!

Sue Whited
Voice II

For Such A Time As This…
…We Are But Small Voices

For Such A Time As This…
…We Are But Small Voices

Deidre B. Hester
Sue E. Whited

MORGAN JAMES

Published by Morgan James Publishing
www.morganjamespublishing.com

ISBN: 0-9746133-3-9

Printed in the United States of America

For Such A Time As This…
…We Are But Small Voices

A true and absorbing look into the lives of two educators. These Christian teachers speak candidly on challenging topics - teachers, parents, students, affirmative action, underachievement, racism - that affect our country today. Join their movement to make a difference where you are for the next generation and beyond!

Deidre B. Hester
Sue E. Whited

For Such A Time As This…
…We Are But Small Voices

Deidre B. Hester
Sue E. Whited

2004

Deidre B. Hester
Sue E. Whited

Dedication

People are sent into our lives for a reason whether they stay for a moment, a season, or a lifetime. When someone is in your life for a reason, it is usually to meet a need you have expressed outwardly or inwardly. They have come to assist you through a difficult time, provide you with help or support, and aid you physically, spiritually, or emotionally. They may seem like a gift from Heaven and they are. They are there for the reason you need them to be. When you figure out why this person is in your life, you will know what you need to do.

This book is dedicated to the One who made it all possible. We give glory and honor to God for all that He has done in helping us to write this book by sending those lifelines we needed to make it happen. We also dedicate it to those people - family members, friends, co-workers - who have shared our lives and made us the people we are today

"Obedience belongs to us; results belong to God."

Deidre B. Hester
Sue E. Whited

For Such A Time As This...
...We Are But Small Voices

Table of Contents

Deidre B. Hester
Sue E. Whited

For Such A Time As This...
...We Are But Small Voices

Chapter I - The Meeting... and More

"I wish that I could repay a portion of the gladness you've strewn along my way. And if I could have one wish, this only would it be: I'd like to be the kind of friend that you have been to me."

- Guest

Voice I: Who would have ever thought that one person could make such a difference? I mean a difference that would create such an impact that I would never have guessed it would happen to me. Yet it has happened to me, and more than once. I believe that God strategically places people in our lives that really make a difference, and I have learned from Maya Angelou to call these individuals that make an impact on us our "lifelines." History has taught us that one person does and can make a difference, either positively or negatively. Consider horrible dictators like Adolf Hitler and Saddam Hussein. It just reminds me to thank the Lord for some of our country's heroes like John F. Kennedy, Martin L. King, Jr., and the main hero who belongs to me as well as millions of other Christians, Jesus Christ, our Lord and Savior. But for me, Sue is one of my favorite and personal heroes who entered my life in the fall of 1990, and this walk of mine has never been the same.

Sue Whited was the name she stated when we first met, and I was impressed by her full, gorgeous set of brown, wavy hair. I

remember her being taller than the average
female and middle aged. Upon further
observation, I saw her put so much
excitement and great exuberance into the
current task at hand that I easily guessed that
she loved teaching. I, on the other hand,
loved the students and was still trying to
acquire a love for teaching, which was not my
first choice of careers. "Now she looks like a
real teacher," I remember thinking as well.
Not that I didn't feel like a real teacher
because I felt I could teach. I just did not
want to teach and had to learn the hard way
that teaching, like preaching, is ordained by
God (Ephesians 4:11). At this time, teaching
jobs were the only doors God would open for
me because He was specifically showing me
how to submit to His will. I don't know how I
looked, but Sue just had that teacher's look
and I noticed it the very first day we met. You
might see her in the grocery store and
correctly guess, "That's a teacher." Even one
of our former students called me over to his
desk one day to show me a picture in a
magazine. "Mrs. Hester", he stated, "Doesn't
that look like Mrs. Whited with that sign -

looking like a teacher-teacher?" Professional decorum disappeared as I fell out laughing while my other students looked on as if I had gone mad. That day "teacher-teacher", a term coined by our former student, was incorporated into my vocabulary.

A teacher-teacher:
- stands up 95% of the time while teaching.
- arrives early to prepare for the day.
- stays late to plan for tomorrow.
- takes work home and actually does it.
- makes detailed lesson plans and grades every project.
- checks to make sure homework is completed.
- spends his/her own money on the students and classroom supplies.
- makes phone calls home to let parents know about problems before it's too late.
- sponsors several activities and/or clubs for the students.

- would rather come in sick than
  have a "sub" fill in for the day.
- has enough sick and personal days
  on the books to retire a few years
  early.
- is selected Teacher of the Year
  every year by someone.

We have all probably known a teacher
who fits that description, but Sue is definitely
one that I know personally. I have often said
to her, "I wish I had you as a teacher in the
eighth grade, and I pray each year for my
children to have a teacher like you." The great
thing about that is how God has done exactly
that more than once.

Sue's initial approach towards me was
warm, friendly, and full of life. I liked her
instantly, and after that one encounter, I felt
myself drawn to her like a moth to a light.
This tall woman appealed to me as sensitive,
experienced, and so full of wisdom. Somehow
I just knew that I would learn from her,
drawing from her like a sponge absorbing
water. Each day we found ourselves engaged
in one-on-one conversation.

I have Sue to thank as the reason why I now vote in each election. I had shared with her on one of those rare occasions when you take a risk with someone you're getting to know and say something deep, straight from the heart. You take this risk with that person and hope they will still like you and consider you an equal after you have said it. Sue taught social studies on our team, so the topic of current events came up often as we talked. Election time was quickly approaching, and Sue wanted to have some type of mock election with our classes (I say "our" classes because in middle school a team of two to four teachers to teach the same group of students in order to plan and correlate lessons/subjects). Needless to say, what two better subjects could you have to work together than language arts, my subject, and social studies? As Sue began to animatedly go over her plans for a mock election during our team planning time, she looked for me to grasp the excitement and tell her what English skills could best be tied into the lesson. As I sat and watched Sue, it was obvious that I was much less enthused than she. "So what do you think?" she asked. Take the risk, I thought, and suddenly my reply just gushed out of me like a child harboring a deep, dark secret. "How am I going to get our students involved in a process I haven't even participated in myself?" Sue looked at me, but not down at me, so from that point I let it all out. I shared with her how as a young black woman; I felt the system was full of mainly white males who held the top positions, with top pay, and we probably would never have a black president because of who I called "the powers that be." I went on to ask, "Why should I vote? I am a nobody in a white man's world." I was bitter indeed, but I sensed Sue's compassionate ear close by as I shared even more and ended with my confession that I had never voted.

By the time Sue finished with me that day, I felt proud to be an American and was ready to vote. As I made plans to register for my first election, I became excited and easily began to think of ways English would tie in perfectly with a mock election. Amazingly, as I look back, it wasn't the gruesome details of dog bites, beatings, or lynchings that caused me to go to the polls. The knowledge of struggles blacks had faced during the Civil Rights movement with the loss of many loved ones and heroes, known and unknown, was still not enough to make me vote. How ironic it was that my good friend, a white woman, had been the most influential in my decision to exercise my 14th Amendment rights. Some people would say that I should be ashamed of being an educator and not voting, but I say it was issues that had stood in the way. God provided a way out for me. Sue was sent into my life for specific reasons, and that was just one of them. Today she is one of the closest friends I have.

On the surface one might be amazed at how our friendship may appear to break some obvious social rules. She is fifteen years my senior and a southern Baptist from a small town in West Virginia. I, on the other hand, am nondenominational (many would say Pentecostal "holy roller"), and a native of Brooklyn, New York. Sometimes I think of myself as a Brooklyn chick because I was born and spent much of my formative years there before my family and I moved to a very small rural area in North Carolina called Gates County. Somehow we found each other, and when we taught together, we made an awesome team that made a positive impact on those we taught and knew, both professionally and personally. This is our story about how we believe God has brought us together for our own personal growth and development, but most importantly, for others. It is our hope that by sharing our story, others can learn and be healed in some small way. We hope the Light that lives within us will be glorified because we have come to realize that even though we are no longer working together, we are still on the same team, with the same goals that will allow our lives to bring glory to Him.

Voice II: In 1990 I was beginning my third year as a middle school social studies teacher and was in the midst of moving to my third room in as many years. It was hot and the air conditioning was not on yet in the classrooms. As my fan whirled loudly, I found myself surrounded by stacks of posters, boxes of books, masking tape, and markers that fourth week of August. Up on a ladder to put yet another poster in just the right place, I heard a voice asking if I knew where a certain room was located. I looked down and there was an attractive, young, black teacher pushing an umbrella stroller with a little girl in it. She introduced herself, and I learned that this was Deidre Hester, my eighth grade team's new language arts teacher. My first impression was: good, we need a black teacher on our team; my second: what a beautiful smile.

Deidre and I seemed to bond almost immediately. She soon became as busy as I was trying to get her room ready. When the four teachers on our team met, she and I seemed to agree as to what we wanted for our students. I was more than willing to help her fit into the school routine and answer any questions she might have. Day after day, we seemed to be together - talking either before or after school, or both. At first glance, we seemed to be an unlikely pair. She was much younger with a year-old daughter, and I was much older, with both of my sons in their twenties. I was raised in West Virginia, and she came from New York City by way of rural North Carolina. Despite our many differences, we soon discovered our most important similarity - we were both Christians. It seemed that our hearts drew us together in a friendship that would overcome race, age, and background.

My experiences with Deidre, both personally and professionally, have impacted my life in a wonderful way. I took a leap of faith in attending church services with her occasionally, and experienced the joy of her church's worship style. I traveled to North Carolina and met her extended family, enjoying some of the best country cooking I've ever eaten. I even asked my husband, Richard, to help with the remodeling of Deidre's and her husband, Larry's home. But most importantly, I was there when their son, Richard's and my godson, Larry Donnell Hester, Jr., was born. Deidre made me a better teacher because what I learned from my friendship with her made me a more knowledgeable and accepting person and was multiplied into many more lives. She became a part of many memorable classroom experiences, helping to inspire our students to achieve. God placed us together for a reason, and even though we no longer work together, we are still working for Him through our sharing, praying, laughter, and tears. What we have together is too good to keep to ourselves, so we are sharing it with you, our readers.

Two Voices As One: Throughout our five years of teaching together, we tried to show our students that "you can't judge a book by its cover," and encouraged them to share their lives and experiences with as many different types of people as they could. Not only did we teach this concept, we modeled it. It was our hope that they would be as blessed as we have been. Now we are taking our story and experiences to another audience - our readers. We hope for the same result as we did with our students.

Chapter II - Teacher to Teacher: Why teach?

"If you have knowledge, let others light their candles at it."

- Fuller

Voice I: "I don't want to teach nobody's 'bad a_ _' kids!" This was what I was thinking when my college English professor suggested that I take education courses since I had already completed my English requirements at the end of my junior year in college. Instead I somehow managed to get out one audible phrase, "If you think so; you're my advisor, so I guess I should." Looking back, I thank God that He delivered me from such filthy language and provided the means for my grammar to improve.

I had come to Livingstone College by chance, or so I thought at the time, to receive my BA in English, and then transfer on to a major university to get a degree in Speech Pathology and Audiology. A doctor by the name of Gaither at Hampton General Hospital was responsible for fostering that desire within me. I had read an article about how he gave people a new lease on life when he would rehabilitate them from near-death experiences after being in car crashes. They would have to have reconstructive surgery and therapy to re-teach them childhood speech and language skills. From that point on, I knew that was what I wanted to do in some form or another. Prior to this I had really planned to pursue a career in acting after undergraduate school, but now this seemed like a more realistic goal. I reminded my advisor that my BA in English would just be a stepping stone to a far greater calling than teaching ever would be. She reminded me that teaching would provide some well-needed funds for graduate school, as well as be something I could "fall back on." With that said, I registered for educational requirements and have been "falling back" on teaching ever since. Really in retrospect, I don't think my distaste for teaching bad kids was the real reason I wanted to avoid teaching. In reality, I just didn't feel competent enough to teach a pet, much less someone else's child. That is why I so strongly feel that teaching was God's plan for my life. Even with so many odds stacked against me, I became the first person in my family to graduate from college, and I did so "cum laude."

I grew up the sixth of eight children in a family whose lives would be torn apart by the separation of a marriage and the death of my father. The result of these experiences left me receiving my formative training at Deauville Gardens Elementary in Long Island, New York, PS 73 in Brooklyn, New York, and

Gatesville Elementary in Gates County, North Carolina. These childhood education experiences left me feeling inadequate, particularly when I moved from Amityville, NY to Brooklyn. Standardized tests dictated that my placement should be in the above average classes. Unfortunately, the principal informed my mother there were no "B slot" classes available, so she could choose to put me in the "A class" or the "D class." Unaware of the detriment this would later cause me, my mother allowed me, at the age of nine, to choose for myself. Looking into the "A Class," I saw lots of hard work, lists of assignments on the board, and students engrossed in books and papers. As I looked into the "D Class," I saw students working puzzles, playing games, and having fun. Is it any wonder that I chose the "D Class?"

This choice had a long-term effect on my educational skills, but somehow the hand of God even turned that to my good because it was in the "D-Class" that I met Mr. Levine. He threw me my first lifeline by encouraging, challenging, and exposing not only me, but also a few others in my class of inner-city children to the life beyond the drug infested, crime-ridden brutal streets of Brooklyn, NY. Somehow Mr. Levine must have intuitively known that we were not meant to be in the "D-Class!" This Sonny Bono look-alike took us to his university when he was working on his Master's degree and exposed us to the life of higher learning. He took us out to eat, on walks through the college campus and the park, and fed us Drake's "devil dogs" while discussing our futures. He also built up our self-esteem by allowing us to perform in plays which he wrote. Of course, I always had a leading role! I remember one play in particular, entitled *Pollution is a Crime*. It featured a song to the tune of "Love Potion #9." I played a character called Smoggy Sam, who thought it profitable to pollute the air with aerosol spray cans. This was my acting debut, and my mother, oldest brother, and uncle were all there. They told me how I was a star performer, and I believed that until high school. This is why I thought my future would involve acting. Yet it was a teacher, Mr. Levine, whose loving nature and caring ways helped me remember years later, how one teacher made all the difference in my life.

I never thought I could be a "Mr. Levine." Yet God's plan would prevail as I was offered a teaching job just two weeks prior to graduating. The Mecklenburg County School system in Charlotte, North Carolina, gave me a contract teaching seventh through ninth grade English classes, contingent on my passing the National Teacher's Exam. I did pass and accepted it as a miracle, since I was accustomed to scoring below the norm on most standardized tests throughout my education. These events allowed me to begin to understand how God really does make the impossibilities of our lives a reality when we do our part.

When I began teaching, I wanted out after just a few years. When I shared this with my pastor, who is also another lifeline of mine, he encouraged me strongly to stay in the teaching field. He said that I should ride out those difficult moments and never quit because God needs His people everywhere, especially in the public school system. It was in 1988 that he said, "One day teachers will receive the pay and respect they deserve." So again, as I had done back in college, I took the advice from a person solely based upon who he was in society and who he was to me. It still would be several years later before I would come to fully realize what Bishop Boone, my pastor and oldest brother, meant. It is God who instills the gift of teaching (Ephesians 4:11 - "It was he who gave some to be… teachers"). Teachers have that gift and are gifts to everyone who has ever received some form of education for any time period or for any reason in their life. I may not have always felt fully competent enough in the academic arena of language arts, but God had chosen me! His choice was enough to give me the motivation to study, work, and practice hard in my content area, and my skills did improve immensely. I discovered I could teach because "I can do all things through Christ who strengthens me." (Philippians 4:13)

Voice **II:** I came to the teaching profession later than most, but I truly believe that I was born to teach. I always enjoyed school as a child. Reading was and continues to be a joy, but math and science required a lot of work on my part. Nevertheless, I always did well in school because I knew that I was expected to do my best and my best was A's and B's. Placed in high academic-tracked classes - they were called "accelerated" in my day - I made a U-turn my senior year of high school and decided that I wanted to go to work after graduation. Whether it was the tumultuous campuses of the mid-1960s or the serious relationship I had with my long-term boyfriend, Richard, I decided that college wasn't for me and changed my math and science classes to business courses. After graduation, I worked in the business sector until my marriage at the very young age of "almost nineteen."

The long-term boyfriend, now my husband, was an airman in the U. S. Air Force and in 1967 we began a 20-year tour of duty at various bases throughout the Southeastern

United States. Two sons, Ric and Bryan, were born to us, and I thoroughly enjoyed being a mother to two very bright boys. From the beginning, I would talk to my babies, teaching them about colors, numbers, and the names of everything we encountered. They were my very first students, and I remember ordering books for them when we really couldn't afford them, believing that books held the key to their futures. I volunteered with the Boy Scouts, became a part-time Sunday School and Bible School teacher, and did the normal "mother" things, like baking cupcakes for school birthday parties and working booths for school carnivals. Whenever I worked in the school setting, I noticed that I really felt invigorated and energized. I enjoyed being there as much as I used to when I was a student, but didn't realize that this was the setting where I should be working until several years later.

After attending junior college part-time in two different states, the boys and I moved home to West Virginia while the military man of our family completed a remote tour of duty in Korea. Once again I tried the business world, working in a job placement agency. I rationalized that it would take a lot of time and money to complete a college degree in nursing or teaching and decided that I should concentrate on secretarial work, enjoying my family and volunteer activities instead. This mind-set worked for the remainder of that year of separation.

When my husband, Richard, returned, he was assigned to Langley AFB in Hampton, Virginia, and within two months of our relocating to this area, I had become a secretary employed in of all places, a school. The first time I walked into Syms Junior High School, it felt right; it even smelled right! I loved the work - it was fast-paced and the teachers, counselors, and administrators were real professionals and fun people with whom to work. After a year or so there, during which I got used to working with students in grades seven through nine, I mentioned to several of the guidance counselors that I thought I would enjoy teaching. They were so supportive that I inquired about evening classes at the local Christopher Newport College. The next five to six years were the most exciting, but exhausting years I had ever experienced in my life. Looking back, I give God the credit for seeing me through such a challenging time. I worked full-time at Syms, which by now had become a middle school with sixth through eighth grade students, and attended classes part-time. I continued to be wife and mom, keeping the house cleaned, the laundry done, the groceries bought, the suppers cooked, and the dogs fed. I know, I should have expected my family to take up the slack, but I was determined that they would not pay for my starting late to complete the degree that I now realized I should have obtained years earlier. I was relentless in my expectations of my college work, using every spare minute to study and prepare. Even the bathroom became a study room, as I would pore over notes in the bathtub and recite speeches in front of the mirror as I curled my hair.

All the hard work paid off in May, 1988, when I graduated Summa cum Laude with a degree in Elementary Education and a concentration in, I believe, the most difficult area to teach, middle school. I graduated already hired - I would teach, not the sixth graders I had requested, but remedial eighth graders - the big guys, most of whom had already failed at least once. I would need my prayers now more than ever! The first year of teaching taught me more than I had ever learned in college about teaching methods, classroom management, parent/teacher communication, and how important my underlying reasons for becoming a teacher really were.

I became a teacher to make a difference in the lives of my students. I have always believed that the subject matter is important, but that my students also need to know about life, values, and consequences of their choices as well. Before the advent of Virginia's SOLs (Standards of Learning), I had more time to dwell on these important "extras," but I still find time to work them into my lessons or the curriculum because, sadly, some of my students will not be exposed to them anywhere else.

When Deidre came on my teaching team, she completed what I started with our students and I did the same for her. We were on the same page, drawing from the same strengths as we held the line on behavior, completion of assignments, and classroom expectations. Unfortunately, not all parents were appreciative of our efforts.

Two **Voices As One:** The teaching profession is an honorable one that affects many lives. Ask anyone you know, and they will remember a particular teacher who changed their life, either for better or worse. The way the teacher spoke, favorite phrases, a particular memorable incident in that class, etc. These memories will go on forever. We believe the most effective teachers are not made; they are born ("We have different gifts… if it is teaching, let him teach," Romans 12:6-7).

Teachers, don't worry that you are not working for a Fortune 500 company or earning a higher paycheck. Don't listen to the nay-sayers who continually criticize the public education system because they aren't talking about you. If you believe that you were born to teach, hang in there! At the end of the day and the school year, you can look back and realize that you were involved in the second most influential career in the world. After parenthood, teachers personally affect the future in powerful ways. You may be the only positive light in a child's life, so don't take your position lightly.

Chapter III - Teacher to Parent

"Children learn best from example;
the trouble is, they don't know a
good example from a bad one."
                                    - Anonymous

Voice I: My desire in this chapter is to send a message to all parents, but in particular, I feel the need to reach out to the black moms in society. So first I simply say to all parents: "Please stop spoiling your child beyond repair because once you begin to defend your child whether he or she is right or wrong or even before you have all the facts, you reinforce the idea that your child does not have to accept full responsibility for his or her own actions."

From a black woman's perspective I have witnessed first-hand, time and time again the mothers of black boys coming to their aid with feathers all ruffled and with a "full cocked barrel," ready to verbally shoot anyone putting the blame on their precious sons. I believe we go into battle for them because we sometimes feel that society has damaged our men, and by acting this way, we're saying "I refuse to be a partaker in also damaging the black male's ego, dignity, and self-respect." We want to shield our sons from the degradation and the shame that has been passed down from generation to generation to our boys from society as a whole. The only problem with this is that our boys become men - men who have not learned that wrong choices have negative consequences, and that mom will not or cannot always be there to defend them.

We need our men to be involved in the lives of our sons. Women can't always successfully rear and train boys, so thank God for the male teachers in our elementary and middle schools. No matter how much a mother wants to raise her son, in reality, it takes a man to make a man and show him by example. I could never teach my son to be a man because I'm not a man. Unfortunately, many single moms don't have an available male to be a positive influence and role model in the lives of their children. In these situations, I would suggest outside activities like scouting, the YMCA, mentoring organizations like Big Brother, and church youth activities where male leadership can help.

My message to all parents is stop making excuses for your sons and daughters. Make them responsible for every action, and hold your child accountable. Take the time from your job and visit their schools. Communicate with their teachers consistently and get to know them. If the teacher tells you they are misbehaving, they probably are. If your student isn't doing his/her work, find out why and become part of the solution, not part of the problem. When you work with the teacher and not against him or her, everyone wins, especially your child.

Voice II: Part of a teacher's job is interacting not only with students, but also with their parents. For some, this is a learned skill; for others, it remains very difficult for a variety of reasons. Moms and dads, single moms or dads, grandparents, and other relatives don't want to hear that "your child is not doing his or her work," "your child is not behaving in class," or "your child is not accepting responsibility." Somehow this is a reflection on them. Some of the most difficult parts of teaching can involve the adults in your students' lives.

If I could speak to the world of parents out there, this is what I would say: "Parents, please allow me to teach your child and hold them accountable for their work and actions. Stop making excuses for them when there are no acceptable excuses!"

Children learn early how to play parent against parent, and once in school, parent against teacher. When that inevitable note or phone call comes, the child is ready with many reasons why the teacher is unfair, prejudiced, or just plain mean. Speaking for myself and many other teachers, I would say that we simply don't have the time to pick on your child. We are too busy trying to teach from one to six classes per day, depending on the grade level. Am I always totally fair? Maybe not, because I am human and can make mistakes. When I do, I try to model the right behavior and apologize to the child in front of the class. How can I expect them to show respect, if I don't lead the way?

Many students have started down the road to ruin because the adults in their lives don't hold them accountable to a high standard of work and behavior. They fight for their child regardless of the situation. The child doesn't learn right from wrong; he/she learns that no matter what they do, mom or others will fight to exclude them from any punishment. Unfortunately that means that the level of misbehavior usually escalates. Situations can worsen and the end result could lie with the police department and the court system. If only parents had allowed the child to take the punishment, learn from the situation, and move on to better and more acceptable behavior. After a certain point, you may have lost a child - one who is expelled from school and begins moving through the revolving door of the juvenile system. What a waste!

Part of life is learning how to deal with different kinds of people. Not everyone is going to treat you fairly, but you have to learn how to work with them. The school can be the first place students learn this lesson in interpersonal relationships. They also learn that not everyone will be your friend, some people can't be trusted, and when you treat people the way you wish to be treated, it feels good. Unfortunately, some students only learn the mantra repeated at home, such as:

"What's in it for me?"

"How dare she touch my child!"
"What do you expect from a
white/black/Hispanic/woman
(put in your own stereotype)
teacher?"

I have always believed that a child learns
what he/she experiences. Living with adults
who are prejudiced, foul-mouthed, nicotine-
or alcohol-addicted, unappreciative or
suspicious of education will lead these once-
innocent young people along the same paths.
Somehow a few overcome negative influences
and that is the reason many teachers continue
in very challenging job situations. They hope
to reach those few precious students and
make a difference in their lives. Are all
teachers perfect and unprejudiced? Of course
not, but most would not have entered the
teaching profession if they didn't have a
caring attitude for and interest in children.
Those who get in for the wrong reasons,
don't last long.

So parents - please work with us to
present a united front for your child. Keep in
touch with your child's teacher(s). While you

have one or more children at home, we have many more in the classroom. Some years my roll book contains 130 or more names. Check with the source - a telephone call or e-mail will allow you to know personal information that will help you at home. Yes, you saw your child working on homework, but did you know that it wasn't turned in to the teacher? Begin writing notes that the teacher will sign and return. That way you will know whether assignments made it to class, what the score was on the last quiz or test, and when the next one is scheduled. If the teacher doesn't respond to your attempts to communicate, keep trying or let the principal know. When parents and teachers work together, the student success rate usually improves. In the long run, your son or daughter will definitely be the winner in that type of educational situation. In conclusion, those parents who told their child, "Your teacher wouldn't have taken the time to call me if something wasn't wrong. What is it?"… have my lasting thanks!!

Two **Voices As One:** Education is a vital part of a child's life. It takes involvement from all sides of the "educational triangle" - student, parent, teacher - to ensure success. In this part of your child's life, parental involvement begins with day one of kindergarten and ends when your son or daughter completes his/her education.

Food for thought: "An ounce of prevention is worth a pound of cure." Would you rather sit in the classroom with your child or in the courtroom?

Deidre B. Hester
Sue E. Whited

Chapter IV - Teacher to Student

"Choice, not chance,
determines destiny."
- Anonymous

Voice II: During my years as a middle school teacher, I have taught children who range in age from ten to fourteen or older, representing the whole spectrum of academic ability and achievement. Every year there are times that I feel the need to speak to my students on a variety of topics. Individually and as a class, I counsel them because it's not easy being a student today. The world is a much more complicated place than when I was a teenager, and today's youth are faced with many more distractions and problems.

Our culture today is definitely not representative of life in the "Ozzie and Harriet" or "Leave It To Beaver" time period. Fewer students are growing up with an intact family consisting of one mother, one father, and one or more siblings. Single parents struggle to financially support their children, sometimes working more than one job and having little personal time to spend with their sons or daughters. Television programs present murder, profanity, disrespect to authority figures, and immoral behavior at all times of the day and night. Music videos show lewd dancing and present lyrics that do not encourage young people to view the opposite sex with respect. The news is filled with depressing events from around the world and just down the street. More and more students come to school with identified and unidentified learning problems. Some come hungry not only for food, but also for attention. It's no wonder that many students are not succeeding in today's classrooms.

In this chapter I want to speak to the world of students who will never enter my classroom and talk to them as though they have:

> "By the time you reach middle school, you are beginning to have a mind of your own. Think about how many times you have disagreed lately with your mom or dad about fashions, music, friends, or even food. At this age you are trying to find yourself and discover who you are. It is very important for you to realize that your life as a teenager will be filled with times when you must make decisions. Some decisions are as simple as which pair of jeans to select from your closet; others are so important that they will impact your future life. Should you listen to your friends who are,

for the most part, just as confused
as you are about what is happening
to their bodies, their thoughts, and
their lives? How about the "cool"
kids or the popular ones - would
they give you good advice? To
whom do you turn when everything
seems to be going crazy? Most of
you, if you're fortunate, have at least
one caring adult who has invested a
lot in you. Think of it - they have
provided a roof over your head,
food on your table, clothes on your
back and in your closet, perhaps a
computer and internet hookup, CD
player, and many other things.

I'm about to mention the
unmentionable: consider trusting
your parents' or guardians' advice.
They have already lived through
your age and have experienced a lot
of what you are going through right
now. They care about you and don't
want to see you hurt. Why would
they give you bad advice? Your
friends or the other young people at

school don't have the same emotional attachment to you that these adults in your life do. So please share with them and seek out their advice. Other adults care about you too. A teacher or counselor that you feel comfortable talking to at school, or a Scout leader or Sunday School teacher could help you with problems as well.

Let me suggest another area of guidance and help. Hopefully, you have been introduced to the One who loves you most and wants to guide you throughout your life. If this concept is new to you, let me give you very good news - you have a Heavenly Father who loves you and has a plan for your life. In Psalms 139 we are told that God knew us before we were born and wants to guide us daily and throughout our lives. He wants only good for us but will allow us to choose our path through life. Learning about this God of the

Ages and His rules for life will definitely help you in making those important everyday choices.

Our society is good at pointing fingers or blaming others for personal mistakes. Regardless of your home situation - two parents, one parent, step-parents, guardians, foster parents, or relatives - you are responsible for the choices you make. You cannot blame anyone else if you choose to not complete your school work or study, run with the wrong type of friends, get involved with cigarettes, drugs, alcohol, or sexual behavior. As motivational speaker Drew Brown says, 'You are the only person you will ever wake up with for the rest of your life.' Make sure that the person looking back at you from the mirror is one who makes you proud, not ashamed. Don't point to anyone else for your mistakes. The Lord gave you a brain - use it! Think before you act, trust those who care for you, and do your best in everything you try. Some chances will only be offered once. You don't want to look back years later and regret passing up a wonderful opportunity.

The bottom line is this: <u>You</u> alone are responsible for your education. Education equals the power not only to qualify for certain jobs, but also to live a more blessed life. No one would turn down a town home to live in the projects, but that could be the result when you say 'no' to school and a better education. Dr. King lived his life trying to open doors that had been closed for many. Teachers come to work everyday just for you. They know the material and simply want to help you along the path to success. Don't slam the door to that path by refusing to be a responsible learner. Every day is a new beginning; use each day wisely because you will never get it back again!"

Voice I: I want to say to all young ladies and gentlemen who are still in school, "keep it real!" As I have said to so many young people already, "Just be yourself."

In reality, the majority of students want so badly to be accepted by their friends in school and other peers they come in contact with on a regular basis, that they assume someone else's identity. That may be just fine as long as you're not doing things that go against your own morals, values, and goals. I strongly suggest that you get to know who you really are. When you are away from your friends, think about yourself:

- What do you like?
- What do you want to do with your life?
- Do you really think that smoking is cool, or sex is

great when no one else is
there to influence you?
-   Do you actually like loud and
talkative people, or do you
prefer a more quiet crowd?

You may discover the peers you want to
accept you are not anything like the real you.
Once you make this discovery, you can feel
less pressure to fit in with that crowd, and
find friends more like yourself. True
friendship should be mostly fun, not mainly
frustrating.

Like most teenagers, my daughter began
to question the values and teachings of our
home. She began to wonder if she believed in
God for herself, or was it because mom and
dad always told her that He was real. She
began to want to wear tight, revealing clothes,
saying it was what she wanted to do, and not
because everyone was doing it. She asked if
she always had to listen to gospel music, or
could she listen to R & B as well? These and
other similar questions began to come up
more and more as she left middle school and
entered high school. My response to her and

to you is that to begin to question and seek your own identity is normal, and you will have to provide the final answers to those questions. To help you do this, watch what happens to the people with positive attitudes, the ones who study, don't do drugs or "drink and drive," versus those who are constantly negative, experiment with illegal drugs, refuse to study, and consume alcohol before they get behind the wheel. Let what you see and know about others help you decide. Remember Michael Jordan didn't become a basketball icon by drinking alcohol, talking and acting "bad," and doing drugs. However Len Bias, college star and the NBA's #1 draft pick tried cocaine once and died in June of 1986.

Students who put name brand dressing and socializing above studying and grades are setting themselves up for failure or the minimum wage lifestyle. When education is not valuable to you, you will come to school just to look good and talk to your friends. Eventually you will come out of school a dummy - how smart is that? Think about this for a moment: have any of you who put so much emphasis on wearing name brand clothes above studying and good grades ever received a commission check for advertising Nike, Tommy Hilfiger, Timberland, and Fubu? If you want to look good, then look good. Just have the brains to back up the good looks!

You will learn that bad things happen to good people, and bad people seemingly have it good. This is a fact of life. The greatest book ever written says "it rains on the just and the unjust" so each person will have hard times in this life no matter how good he/she is. Significant to that truth is how we go through the bad times. Will you turn to drugs, alcohol, or sex to appease your hurt or will you turn to God and your family and friends who care? Can you look in the mirror and honestly say, "I like the person looking back at me?" Will you feel good about yourself whether you have one friend or twenty? Once again, I want to stress to you that you must be true to yourself. Find a way to do that and just stay "real."

Many of you have read S. E. Hinton's, *THE OUTSIDERS* and remember Johnny's character telling Ponyboy to "stay gold" as

Johnny lay dying. Gold will still be gold, even when it has gone through fire. To your parents and others who care for you, you are gold and precious. Stay true to their teachings and don't let others change you from a precious gem to a ruined stone. If you can live with your decisions, that is all that matters. Regret is a painful experience, and some decisions change our lives forever and we can never take them back.

In conclusion, remember to make the most out of your life. You need to make every moment count because tomorrow is not promised to you, so make today your best day. Choose to be positive, and treat people the way you want to be treated. It is so important that you set goals for your life and then work to reach them. Today is your chance to make it all happen. I just know you can succeed if you keep trying. Never give up or stop trying to make yourself better. Keep improving yourself until the day you die. Now get ready, get set, and go do it!

Two **Voices As One:** You may not realize it, but school is just one small portion of your life. Set goals, decide now what you want to do in life, and "go for it!" Remember that being successful in school will help you be successful in life. Bill Gates, one of the richest men in the world because of his knowledge and inventive work with computers, once said, "Get to know and make friends with the nerds in your school - one day they may be your bosses!" Put equal emphasis on your looks and academic ability. Being "cool and cute," but in reality, "dumb and despondent" is such a waste of your life. As a student, you must understand that ignorance is more expensive than knowledge because "not knowing" will affect your potential earnings for the rest of your life. It is possible to look good, be popular, and be smart at the same time. <u>A well-rounded person is a fantastic package!</u>

Deidre B. Hester
Sue E. Whited

Chapter V - Overworked, Underpaid, and Misunderstood

"Teachers are the heart of learning because they make hope happen."
- Anonymous

Voice II: Who in the world would go to college for four years to earn a degree in one or more specific subjects, then continue on for another year to

51

acquire their certification? Education majors - teachers - that's who. Then after five years of higher education, these men and women of all ages, races, and backgrounds enter the "real world" of students, administrators, parents, computer grade programs, lesson plans, deadlines, standardized testing, telephone and face-to-face conferences, meetings, blame and accusations. They probably ask themselves, "What have I gotten myself into?"

The teaching profession is a sometimes challenging, but often very rewarding career. However, those on the outside have no idea of how difficult it can be to attempt to motivate, teach, test, remediate, retest, and grade students from age five to nineteen in class sizes ranging from 10 to 35 or more students at a time. Those teachers who excel at their job usually begin their day at least half an hour before the students arrive, teach one class all day in various subjects, one subject all day to five or more classes, or a variety of classes to even more than five sets of students. They have very few bathroom or rest breaks throughout the day. At lunchtime, they gulp down their food while sometimes supervising children, dashing to the copy machine, helping students with makeup work, or answering telephone messages. Then they stay after the children have left for the day to tutor certain students, gather up work, enter grades in the computer, plan for tomorrow or next week, and attend faculty meetings, conferences, or workshops. If this weren't enough, most teachers end their day at school by loading up all the papers, projects, or mail they haven't been able to complete or read in a big carry-all bag to take home. Getting through this bag might take an additional one to two hours, and then they can look forward to doing it all again the next day. The teaching profession can definitely be described as one in which the employees are overworked, and those entering the profession can expect to earn the whopping starting salary of $28,000+ a year. Teachers are underpaid!

Teachers across the country in all disciplines with all age groups are characteristically underpaid. Somehow this low paycheck seems to demonstrate a lack of respect for the profession. I've listened to talk radio or read articles criticizing teachers and stating the opinion that they are paid enough already. These pundits talk about the three months off every summer (actually less than that), the short work day (8:30 to 2:30 - not quite!), and the fact that teachers really don't have to work very hard. I just have to laugh, but actually such statements are sadly out of touch with reality. One internet story told the tale of a derisive parent who said that teachers deserve no more pay than the amount a babysitter would earn. Once the math was completed, the amazed parent realized that paying only 50 cents per hour per student would total a yearly salary of over $100,000 a year - a sum no classroom teacher currently earns. That humorous story aptly illustrates the current teacher salary situation. Basic babysitter pay from the 1960s would multiply the average teacher salary almost three times! Do teachers deserve more pay? I remember listening to parents after they have volunteered in the school for a day or so. I would see them shake their heads in amazement at how much teachers have to accomplish every day and see their disappointment at the attitudes, disrespect, or just plain apathy shown by some misguided students. Usually they make some sort of comment, such as: "I don't know how you do it; the public ought to see what teachers have to experience with other people's children!" Those volunteers appreciate us and think we deserve more money because they have been on the front line with us. A saying I found on a refrigerator magnet states another truism: "Parents appreciate teachers the most when it rains all weekend." Teachers are underpaid!

You cannot truly understand another person's perspective unless you have experienced their situation firsthand (Ch. VII - Two Voices As One). For that reason alone, teachers are misunderstood. Some parents don't understand that we teach more than just their child, and cannot give Susie or Hector extra-special treatment. A teacher has to be seen by their students as fair, someone who treats all students equally. Unless an identified condition or disease deems this child worthy of special treatment, a teacher has to apply the classroom rules equally to each and every child in his/her class. Deadlines are another area that some parents find difficult to understand. If a project or an assignment is due by a certain date, then points are deducted from the grade for work that is turned in later. If you know that there is a conflict (appointment, trip, etc.), communicate that problem early and then misunderstandings can be avoided.

A teacher can be misunderstood by his/her administrator if the lines of communication are not kept open. I have heard horror stories about domineering and dictatorial principals who don't enter the classroom to see what and how the children are learning, but come to "knit-pick" and check off every little detail on bulletin boards, learning centers, and lesson plans. These type of people don't lead, they dominate and they make the teaching profession a living hell for the teachers at that particular school. They need to go because they do no one any good. Thankfully I have not experienced any principals like the ones described above. I have worked with ten or more principals during my teaching career, and although they each had different styles, they were all caring, open, and willing to listen. Possibly our positive relationships were due to the fact that I was a hard worker doing my job, but I have to give them credit for being people that I was willing to follow because their demands were fair and impacted positively on the students I taught.

The most misunderstanding sometimes comes from the central office - those who I characterize as working in the "ivory towers." These people never experience our lives firsthand, but have no problem whatsoever in dreaming up more and more criteria and paperwork for us to complete. Superintendents, assistant superintendents, curriculum leaders, and others are so far removed from the classroom that there are many instances where misunderstandings can readily occur. My suggestion for the problem is to require everyone - even the superintendent - to periodically enter the classroom to plan, teach, grade, discipline, and communicate to parents, not just for a day, but for 3-4 weeks. Once they have been reminded of the reality of the "real world," communication would be reinstated and more understanding of the teacher's situation regained.

The media really seems to have the teaching situation skewed. Numerous articles and talk shows have attacked the public school system and unqualified teachers who are "failing our students." As long as students are passed to the next grade year after year without acquiring the reading, writing, and math skills necessary to master that grade level's work, the system will be broken. Many states have these types of rules or allow parents to manipulate existing criteria so that their child is promoted regardless of low test scores or failing report card grades. Occasionally, the Superintendent or others will make an executive decision to silence a complaining parent and allow a retained student to move to the next grade. Middle school students reading on a third grade level move on to sixth or seventh grade unable to understand the textbooks and unwilling to do the work because they haven't had to in the past. It's not just the schools and the teachers who are part of this seemingly broken system because the parents, students, legislators, and others share in the blame. However, the result is the same - too many students who lack the basic skills to succeed or move to the next level. Accountability is being focused solely on one side of this problem. I have always maintained that the teacher - me - is only one third (1/3) of the problem or the solution. The rest of this "school math problem" - the student and the parent - make or break the education equation. This situation can also be explained in an analogy of a three-legged stool. Each leg is crucially important if the stool is to support any weight. Remove any leg, and the stool collapses.

For these and other reasons, teachers are often misunderstood. However, many of us wouldn't do anything else for a living. We find that the hard work is worth it when we see the light in a student's eyes when he/she finally catches a concept and smiles broadly, or hear the gratefulness in a parent's voice as they thank us for the extra tutoring we have done for their child. At the end of the day, I feel satisfied because I am a part of one of the most honorable of professions - I am a teacher!

Voice I: Notably, the teaching profession is one of the most honorable and influential of jobs, but not all Americans realize that. They also don't understand the problems with some of our flawed educational systems that are unduly challenging teachers as well as students.

It is a known fact that our educational systems are of great concern to many people. We often hear about efforts being made to help promote change for the better by our lawmakers and school officials. Yet sometimes, the very people working towards these changes tend to be, in my opinion, the wrong people. This is because some of the people making the decisions for the current teachers have been out of the classroom for long periods of time, or worse still, have never taught at all. The question is how can they know what is best or what is needed? I feel strongly that we need to stop putting Band-Aids on our problems within the educational system and instead perform major surgery to fix the wounds.

We are facing some serious educational issues in our country today. For example, we are living in the 21st century and involved with a high tech era that is rapidly growing, forcing us to compete with other countries. Will our students, who are also our future, be prepared? Perhaps it is time to revamp our entire system. Long gone are the days when one teacher stood and taught a group of kids that outnumbered him/her. Laura Ingalls Wilder of the *Little House on the Prairie* series could do this well because the caliber of students was so different. However, today one person meeting the educational, psychological, and emotional needs of 27+ children seems ridiculous. Sometimes not having enough textbooks for each student or even a classroom in which to prepare and teach is a reality for some in the profession. Not to mention the fact that daily some students come to school with guns or drugs or are totally uninterested in learning. This is a new millennium that presents teachers with many new and challenging problems.

For these problems there are no easy answers, but we are still not close to addressing all of the issues. This is because society has failed to consult the experts in this matter, the teachers who are involved on a day-to-day basis. Some people say, "Teachers are underpaid and I couldn't or wouldn't do their jobs - give them a raise!" But that's a simple way out. I believe it is time for society as a whole to become more knowledgeable and get involved with the educational process. Each adult needs to feel responsible for helping to educate our students because, as President Herbert Hoover said years ago, "Children are our most valuable natural resource." Yet we don't seem to want to involve ourselves with really preparing them even though we know how important they are to our future.

Some students will never make it on just "book knowledge;" they may need to pursue a vocation. What would be wrong with some students earning a vocational diploma instead of being passed, but not promoted, through the system year after year? Many teachers object to these "administrative promotions," but are often overruled and then ultimately blamed for students not graduating with basic skills. I feel we need to have more vocational, technical trade, college prep, and life skills schools in every school system where students can learn a skill or trade so they can be taught to be an asset to society and not a burden. Such schools would enable a student to achieve and succeed in areas that are excluded in most current systems. Each student should have a choice in his/her future plans and not be forced to fit into a curriculum that is not of their choosing. The major misunderstanding in most school systems today is assuming that all students must follow an academic track in high school to prepare for college. For some students this process is similar to trying to force a square peg into a round hole because not all students are college material. Robert White, a great educator, once said, "<u>Every</u> child needs to feel success." How then do we help every child to be successful? We do this by addressing their needs and not ours. If society does not allow some students to succeed outside the academic realm, they will fail within it.

Students today are getting mixed messages. The school expects our youth to attend class after class, listening to lecture after lecture, be quiet, take notes, and make good grades. Yet everything else in society tells them to express themselves, have fun, and be spontaneous. Nintendo, Game Cube, DVDs, CDs, and computers have replaced kickball, street hockey, family nights out, and "red light, green light, 1-2-3." With less outdoor and physical recreation time, it is no wonder that teachers have more discipline problems, need to counsel and help students work out personal situations, and find themselves filling out loads of paperwork - all of which cut into actual teaching time.

Our society needs to understand that it's not just the schools or the teachers that affect our students. The homes from which they come can also influence the children who find their way into our classrooms. Many moms and dads in two-parent homes have little time to spend there because their budget or lifestyle requires two incomes. Single parent homes leave many students home alone from the precious hours of 3:00 p.m. until 11:00 p.m. Who is home to enforce homework time, house rules, and train the child in the way he should go? (Proverbs 22:6) Even when two parents are in the home, the demands of living in the 21st century with church, clubs, civic groups, recreation leagues, grocery store lines, mall shopping, and the excessive number of social obligations (birthday parties, anniversaries, showers, etc) allow children too much "alone time." Many times they don't have to conform to rules at home, but are expected to follow rigid rules at school. The teachers and principals become the enforcers with parents many times not understanding why their child is being disciplined and treated "unfairly."

It is a sad day when one can make millions shooting a ball or just throwing one, while a teacher may have to work two jobs just to make ends meet. This may send a message to our youth that education is really not important to make a good living. Likewise, it keeps teachers demoralized as they get the message, "Just keep them in class, help them pass the state required tests, and we will pay you something for your trouble." Have we mixed up our priorities in the pursuit of material possessions? Have we forgotten that investing in human lives was and still is one of our greatest responsibilities? Or could the problem lie with the fact that the majority of Americans just don't understand?

Two **Voices As One:** America needs to know and realize that we must all accept the responsibility for the well-being of our future generations. The teachers and the school system cannot do it all. Education does not begin or end inside the classroom or the school building. It will take a "village" and more to help rear our children. Wake up America - our children need us! We must stop being blind to their needs as we so selfishly pursue our own. Things do not replace parenting - a telephone, computer, TV, and DVD player cannot raise your child and can interfere with his/her education. What we <u>leave in</u> our children in terms of character, morals, and lessons for life is much more important than what we <u>give to</u> them. This is not a racial thing, a gender thing, or a cultural thing - it is a people thing. We all need to understand that we must come together on some common ground and put our differences aside to work for the good of all of our children. As teacher/astronaut Christa McAuliffe once said, "I teach - I touch the future."

So does society and so do parents.

Deidre B. Hester
Sue E. Whited

Chapter VI - People (and Sometimes We) Just Don't Understand

"To lead others out of darkness,
let them see your light."
- Anonymous

Voice II: After Deidre and I became close friends, we would occasionally go shopping at the mall, check out materials at school supply stores, or eat out at local restaurants. Many times we would see some of our students while we were in these social situations. They usually seemed amused to see the "dynamic duo" together outside the classroom as well as side by side at school. However, we rarely got such a positive reaction from some adults who observed us in the public setting.

People just have to understand that Deidre and I enjoy being together. We laugh a lot as we discuss things that happen at school or with our families, finding humor in most of the situations life throws at us. As we walked through the mall, laughing, joking, and sharing, you couldn't imagine some of the looks we got from people observing our interaction. Black women in particular seemed to be perturbed as they glanced our way. Their rolled eyes seemed to say, "What could those two be so happy about, and why are they shopping together anyway?" We've noticed the looks, the body language, and expressions, but choose to go our merry way, figuring that they just don't get it. They don't understand that our friendship is real and close because we truly care about one another and our families.

I've also had occasion to go out in public with Deidre's husband, Larry. Once when I traveled with the family to Washington, D.C. to support one of the children's activities (I am the godmother, you know!), Larry and I were the first ones ready to go out the next morning. I went with him to get breakfast for the whole group and we stopped at both a fast food restaurant and a grocery store before returning to our hotel. At both places, the eyes were checking us out - Larry, younger and black, and me, older and white. We ignored the reactions, not even speaking of it, but Larry later shared with Deidre that he was very aware of people's interest in us at both public places.

These brief experiences have given me some perspective on the challenging situations some people live with permanently because they have chosen to marry someone of a different race. The eyes are always on them, comments made just within earshot, and seemingly constant surveillance from surrounding people in every public situation.

Even though such marriages are increasing in number, they are still enough of an oddity that they bring out the curious nature of those who are inclined to stare and gossip. One of my former students who is a fraternal twin from a mixed marriage (black father and white mother) told me that she and her sister are always getting stares when they are out in public with one or both of their parents. One woman was bold enough to ask her mother who "those children were she was with?" I don't know how polite a reply I could manage in that situation, especially when it might be the 199th time it has happened. Why don't people understand that we live in a time when some of us are able to see beyond race, color, or culture to love another person. How much better the world would be if more people could live in like manner. Instead of looking for perceived differences, why not embrace our similarities?

I may be white and some people might be quick to say that I "don't understand," but I will never understand the inequity surrounding the use of the "N" word. I am not inclined to use this unacceptable term for black people which Mr. Webster's dictionary defines as an "ignorant, uneducated person." The definition goes on to say that this word is only acceptable in "black English," a statement with which I do not agree at all. I don't feel it is a term anyone should use. I know if I ever did say this word in public, the disdain of everyone within earshot would be evident unless I was attending a Klan rally! Intelligent white people just don't use that term to describe blacks. It was a name given to slaves and newly-freed men and women by those who would build themselves up by lowering others through discrimination. I hate that word! It stirs up images of lynchings, cross burnings, and cowardly whites who hid their identities in hooded robes. Why in the world would such a word become a part of African-American slang, rap lyrics, and movie dialogue? Why is it acceptable for gangsta-style music, young blacks and their white counterparts to greet one another with the phrase, "What's up, my nigga?" I will never get it - how in the world can it be unacceptable for me to use it, but accepted and embraced by your good friend who shares your color? Society as a whole just doesn't understand how divisive this historical, but hurtful word is. In my opinion, a term that divides us instead of uniting us should never be acceptable to anyone.

Another issue that puzzles me is how the public as a whole doesn't understand the uniqueness of the relationships that sometimes develop between a teacher and his/her students. Some students always become closer to you than others, but sometimes circumstances forge a student's face and name into your memory forever. After almost twenty years as a classroom teacher, I can name several memorable students:

- There was Sean, the class clown with gorgeous, curly brown hair, who could easily disrupt a whole class with only a funny look and did so many times during my first year as a teacher.

- In that same class was Ira, a troubled underachiever, who couldn't believe that I came to one of his after school basketball games. I met his mother and little sister there in the gym. He was gunned down in the streets and died several years later.

- Then there was Elton, who had many talents, but also many problems and is now serving a life sentence in prison for a death he caused in a drive-by shooting. In my mind, I can still see a beautiful poster he made for a "I Have a Dream" project.

- With a tear in my eye, I remember Carlton, an especially precocious and handsome young man, who drove all the girls crazy in the eighth grade. He had an inner, spiritual quality that really drew me to him. I went to one of his Saturday morning football games the year I taught him and met his family, including his mom who was expecting another child that year. After graduation from high school, he and his cousin were shot and killed in a rural area not too far from our city. Going to the funeral home with Deidre was a very difficult thing to do. It was such a tremendous loss of an incredible young life, and such heartache among so many of his peers. A few years later I would have his sister in my class, the child his mom was carrying when I attended that Saturday morning game so many years earlier. His family and I had come full circle.

- It was Tameka who caused much hysteria and many tears among her female classmates when she left school early to go to the hospital and give birth to her baby on the very day of the eighth grade dance. Her pain upon leaving the building early with other upbeat classmates who were also leaving early to get their hair done for the dance did more to reinforce the concept of birth control or abstinence than any Family Life lecture.

- Several years ago it was Charles who was his family's pride and joy. The oldest son, he was a model student who came back to the classroom as a young teacher. I gasped in shock early one morning as I saw his picture in the newspaper, arrested on an assault charge. The disappointment I felt for him and his family was almost unbearable as I reflected on how prominently this article was displayed. It was almost as if the reporter and newspaper took joy in documenting a teacher charged with such an offense. It seems that when a teacher is charged with a crime, "innocent until proven guilty" is rarely assumed.

- Finally there was Emile who died during his eighth grade year under suspicious circumstances. He was in my homebase class, one of twenty-eight students. I found out about his death merely by chance after stopping in the neighborhood where flashing lights and police cars seemed to be everywhere. When I asked an officer who was investigating an obvious crime what had happened, he identified the home where he said a young man had died. I went home to check my student info, never believing that the tragedy could have affected one of my students. But it had and did affect numerous others who couldn't believe that one of their classmates had actually died. That endless week of talking, counseling, crying, and finally speaking at his funeral, was one I will never forget.

Teaching is not just about curriculum, homework, standardized testing, and report cards. It's also about relationships and memories. The public sometimes doesn't understand how these types of incidences weigh heavy on your shoulders and in your heart. Somehow you have to keep your emotions together, stay strong for your students, and continue to do your job when inside you just want to scream out that life is not fair! For all the wonderful relationships and positive experiences that bring up your spirits as a teacher, there will be those that drag you down and crush you to your core. Believe me, prayer works and sometimes that's all I had to keep me going, but it was enough.

So the next time you drive by your neighborhood school, please remember to whisper a prayer for those inside. The students represent many families, and the teachers and other adults in the building are there doing a difficult job, forming relationships that you may never understand.

Voice I: It's a Black thing, you wouldn't understand" and "The Blacker the college, the sweeter the knowledge" were popular quotes worn on t-shirts by many of our black students during the late 1980s and early 1990s. Today I say it's a "people thing" and we'd all better try to understand before it's too late.

At that time in our careers, Sue and I would marvel at the boldness of the blacks who proudly wore such clothing. Sue had frequently commented about how whites would be considered racists if they had worn similar statements with the word "White" instead. As a matter of fact, her son, Bryan, considered having such a shirt made, but when Sue suggested that he do it, he reconsidered, saying, "I'd probably get my butt kicked!"

My response back then was that it was just blacks displaying pride in our heritage. After all, blacks had not been able to go to many of the white Ivy League schools and major universities for decades. These traditional black universities, one of which I had attended, enabled black students to obtain higher education when they would have been rejected by other schools because of low SAT or other scores. Although I wasn't brazen enough to buy and wear such a shirt, I felt some pride in the list of schools printed on the backs of the "sweeter the knowledge" shirts because my college, Livingstone College, was listed among them. I further stated to Sue how I felt some whites had displayed racism for years with the wearing of the Confederate flag and the slogan inscribed underneath, "The South is gonna rise again." Additionally, when blacks began wearing the X symbol, made popular by Spike Lee's autobiography film about Malcolm X, whites responded with a shirt that read, "You wear your X and I'll wear mine" (the X on this shirt was the symbol of the Confederate flag).

We also commented on the irony of how we had met at Jefferson Davis Middle School, which is now called Davis Middle School in order, I think, to be "politically correct." Years ago the school's band even had grey uniforms reminiscent of the South's Civil War military garb, and their mascot was called, of all things, the Rebel! Believe it or not, this was as recently as the early 1980s, but today Davis proudly displays a colorful and very muscular Bulldog to everyone's delight. Sue was white and from the South (if you consider WV a part of the original VA south), while I was black and from the North. Who could have ever imagined that our very own 20th century version of the Civil War (school can be a battle zone!) would occur in an American classroom where we both would teach and close our ranks to an even playing field by finding success in education.

Despite the civil rights advancements ending segregation and discrimination in public schools, the tension between the races still exists on a large scale, and HEAR THIS WELL: blacks can be racist too. Yes, it is true and it is only when we accept the fact that many of us are, or were, or just have some racist attitudes that the healing can really begin. Again, it is the truth that sets us free. Another truth that I must admit is that I probably had more racist attitudes than Sue did.

Sue is just one of those unique people who take others for who they are and doesn't judge according to color. She often says, "Color is not a problem - just do what you are supposed to do." However, I still had some bitter feelings toward the white community, but Sue's influence and love helped me move through those feelings and lose long-held resentment. What made our relationship so special was that, despite our differences, we both loved people and shared a desire to pull out the best qualities in our students so they could realize their greater potential. Most importantly, we both loved God and wanted to not only hear and speak His word, but also live it as well.

I once told Sue that it was easy for her not to be bitter or feel hate because she did not have to walk around in a brown package and feel the adverse effects that came from wearing a black "earth-suit." However, I did not know that she had family members who had suffered reverse discrimination and acts of "black on white" crime. She called them to task and held them to right saying, "Remember, that this is just some blacks, not all of them," while I thought of the many people I knew who still said, "White people are this," or "Those people are that." That's what I mean - in spite of what happened or happens, Sue won't make excuses for either side. She expects the same from all of us - our best - regardless. So it is no wonder that when I was with Sue out in public, I felt totally at ease. I would laugh with her, hug her, kiss her on the cheek or pat her back without reservation because I felt free and totally accepted by her. When I was with Sue, I'd totally forget that racial tension and misunderstanding existed. Yet, when I would get the stares from other black females, I was reminded how, I believe, black women seem to have the hardest time coping with mixed relationships.

Some black women were already bitter because black men still seemed to want white women even after the brutal history of tortures, lynchings, and ridicule experienced in years past by those who dared to speak, touch, or even look at a white woman. Additionally, black women sometimes felt rejected by their own when black males experienced a high level of success or "finally made it," and chose mates from outside the race as a part of the successful image package. Perhaps black women also felt threatened because they rationalized that if white women take "our" men, we may have to consider theirs for possible mates. The looks from these women seemed to say, "What is wrong with that sister? Is she also cheating on the race by being friends with a white woman?" The looks only encouraged me to hug Sue a little harder and a little longer. Perhaps they'd get bold enough to ask and I would be brave enough to say, "This is a God thing and unless you're one of His, you'll never understand."

Believe it or not, during some of the same conversations when Sue and I discussed those bold t-shirt designs, we also discussed and almost argued about that "N" word. Sue's position was "I just don't get it," while I felt that blacks' acceptance of that term among themselves came from the past. During slavery times, whites called Africans "niggers," and the name caught on among the slaves themselves. For example, a house slave who held a higher position on the plantation might refer to a field hand by the term he heard most often used. Today we still use phrases like, "What's up, my nigga" or "Nigga, please," or "Nigga, you trippin' "to our closest friends and relatives. It's as if we are saying, "If that's all others can see in me, I'll use and even capitalize from it. I'll use it as if that word can't hurt me."

There was a time that I used it in my family, but as I grew older I realized the detriment I was bringing to myself and other African-Americans and knew I had to stop using that word. Again I say this word is in our history and will continue to perpetuate itself unless exposed and honestly discussed. It reminds me of a young man in an Oprah Winfrey special entitled "The Color of Melanin" who asked why his buddies used that word to refer to each other. "Why don't we say 'What's up, my friend?' or 'What's up my fine, young African-American?' This was a name given to us by slave masters. Why use it? It has been said that "children learn what they live," and "we become what we are called." This fact alone should force us to stop using that word. If that's not enough, remember God's word which states, "We are beautifully and wonderfully made." That does not describe a nigger!

Another thing that people just don't understand is that teachers can and do bond with their students in many positive ways. So I want people to realize that after countless days of teaching and interacting with a particular student, you can build a rapport that can last a lifetime. I can still remember the first time I ever experienced the loss of a student. Sue and I both taught him. Emile was bold and outspoken, but likeable. He was one who had lots of potential, but needed attention and encouragement to overcome some negativity. One Friday he was there; by Monday, he was gone. I remember how I hugged him in the hall on his way to the buses that last day. I told him I was proud of the job he had done in the eighth grade talent show when he had sung "It's So Hard To Say Goodbye To Yesterday." How ironic his choice of music had been. It was almost as if this song had prophesied his untimely end from a gunshot wound. He died just as the main character, Cochise, did in the 1960 movie "Cooley High" from which the song Emile had sung was taken. The only difference was that the movie character was killed in the streets while Emile was found dead at home. They said it was suicide, but I never accepted that explanation.

Not long after Emile's loss, Sue and I experienced the death of another student - Carlton - who was brutally gunned down in a remote field away from home. I remember how he listed Sue as his favorite "white" teacher and me as his favorite "black" teacher in the yearbook. He was such a good looking and talented kid, and his death was such a waste. People said he was in the wrong place at the wrong time, but we'll never know.

Years later I lost another student, Albert, to a gunshot wound. He was killed by a home-made gun and died in his father's lap, never even getting to go to high school.

Finally, there was Devon, who was one of my greatest losses because I had pleaded with the principal to let him come back to school. While suspended, he was killed in a car accident. There were three in the car, but he was the only one killed. It hurt so much because I felt he was one who could have made it, but he slipped through the system. As much as I tried to help him, I couldn't change what happened. Even as I reflect on these losses, it still hurts.

Speaking as a person and as a teacher, I want to try and help people understand all of the things that I have shared in this chapter. My response to everyone is to get over your prejudicial, judgmental attitudes and start trying to understand that we all are people first, and races or cultures second! Be willing to open your life to a friend of whatever ethnic group you desire, and move beyond your race, culture, and comfort zone. You don't have to force it; it will come to you naturally. After all, God allows situations to come to us that help us to grow, but the choice to engage will always be ours. I would encourage you to be open to people of other races now, because in Heaven there will be no color lines.

Two Voices As One: Of all the things that people don't understand, I guess we want to emphasize the uniqueness of the student/teacher bond. It has been said that "teachers touch the future," but we feel that students definitely touch teachers' hearts. They also have a way of reaching out and teaching us many things in different ways. One of the most important things we can learn from students is how to care and love unconditionally. The best educators anywhere can tell you that students don't really care how much you know until they can tell how much you care. Looking back we realize that some student/teacher relationships continue even after death, because we will never forget them.

Although the events mentioned in this chapter are true, student names were changed in order to ensure their protection and privacy.

Deidre B. Hester
Sue E. Whited

Chapter VII - We Agree to Disagree

"Each man can interpret another's experiences only by his own."

- Thoreau

Voice II: Coming from two very different backgrounds, Deidre and I sometimes disagree on topics in the news or life in general. She will see a totally different scenario than I expected, or I will offer some insight that she hadn't considered.

But some topics just seem to have no middle ground, so for the sake of our relationship, we have "agreed to disagree."

Affirmative Action

As a white, middle class educator, I am all about fairness, hard work resulting in positive rewards, and equal access. However, when I read stories about affirmative action conflicts in the 21st century, I just don't get it! The years since the Civil Rights legislation of the 1960s and beyond should have equaled the playing field for people of color. Why then is it necessary to push for minority hiring, college admittance, etc.? The Supreme Court must have been thinking along the same line when they decided in June, 2003, that the University of Michigan could not assign additional points or use a quota system for African-American students when considering their applications for admittance. In my opinion, affirmative action seems to be a "reverse discrimination" situation or an obvious put-down to African-Americans. It leads to the mind-set that this is the only way people of color can make the grade; that they have to be given advantages because of perceived deficiencies. I don't think this type of backlash thinking was the intention of affirmative action in the first place, and I don't agree that it was meant to be a never-ending program that blacks and others can count on for all time. Not all minorities agree with this system either. Former NFL football star, minister, and writer, Reggie White, calls the affirmative action system "broken," and states in his book *BROKEN PROMISES, BLINDED DREAMS* that "as long as man looks to man for help instead of looking to his Heavenly Father, he is doomed to fail." African-American editorial columnist, Leonard Pitts, Jr., writes a message to me and others who agree with my way of thinking by saying, "If affirmative action is defined as giving someone an extra boost based on race, white men have always been the biggest beneficiaries of affirmative action since slots for academic admission, bank loans, and public office have routinely been set aside for them over the years." Mr. Pitts goes on to say that "those of us who fail to believe that race is not a significant factor in white success are simply delusional." I might have to disagree with him based on personal experience.

In the early 1990s, I saw how affirmative action affects non-minority students seeking scholarships when my youngest son attempted to qualify for tuition assistance for college. He was told that although his GPA was high and he qualified in other areas, he needed to be a minority to be eligible for the help he sought. Needless to say, that policy and comment left a bad taste in his mouth and gave me a new perspective on government guidelines in this area.

In the business sector, the result of affirmative action type of hiring and supervision has resulted in what I believe to be flawed thinking by company leaders and legal advisors. The unwritten rule that I have heard goes as follows: don't even think about dismissing a black employee, a woman, or other minority without undeniable proof which represents weeks to months of paperwork. It doesn't matter if the person is incompetent, breaks the rules, loses money, comes in late, or has no people skills in dealing with the public or other workers. The perceived reason behind the dismissal or even a temporary suspension will be racism or discrimination. This is the playing card of choice for many in the above categories. Somehow these people do not have the capacity or have never learned to evaluate the reason for the disciplinary action and look within themselves for a problem that needs fixing. The boss is obviously a racist or hates women! The sad part of this situation is that the legal representation for many corporations has fallen right in line with this type of thinking. In order to prevent frivolous lawsuits, managers and supervisors are instructed to placate workers and prevent problems by managing these people in such a way as to avoid any conflicts. This unwritten job description is almost impossible to accomplish. The problems continue with more and more co-workers coming to the conclusion that minorities are protected regardless of what they do, but those of the white/male population need not apply for the same treatment. Once again, I just can't understand or approve. I have always felt that each person should be judged by his or her own actions, and held accountable for the same. If anyone wants equal access, then they should play by the same rules. Equality is earned, not given.

<u>Group Identity</u>

I have lived in an urban area of southern Virginia for over twenty years and have interacted with many races of people in many different settings. Through the years, I have noticed an interesting phenomenon among different groups of African-Americans which I choose to call "Group Identity."

Throughout this book, you may have noticed that Deidre refers to the black race, black, women, and black families as "we." I had heard her use this term for years, but as we worked on this book, the reality of the differences between how I viewed my race and the way in which she saw hers became much more vivid to me. I wondered why we viewed people, especially from our own races differently? I rarely even call members of my own extended family by the pronoun "we," but she includes a whole race of people and uses the term frequently. I guess I'm more of an individualist, rationalizing that in this life, I am only responsible for me, not my brother, my co-worker who looks like me, or the white criminal who ate his victims!

I have also noticed that when I teach the topic of slavery to students as young as eleven or twelve years of age, I hear the same thing from African-American youngsters. "Why did they treat *us* that way?" "*We* should have never accepted slavery!" These sixth graders personalize this unfortunate part of our history, seeming to really feel a part of it themselves. What happened in the past is remarkably real to them. I guess I could compare it to how some of today's Jewish population view the Holocaust.

Perhaps this is why some African-Americans seem loathe to criticize members of their own race for actions that should easily be viewed as inappropriate, unacceptable, or just wrong. For example, a few years ago, a group of black high school boys were videotaped running through the stands at a football game, beating up on people, and causing a near-riot. To their defense came the <u>Rev.</u> Jesse Jackson, making excuses for what they had done, and saying they were only being prosecuted because of their race. It was obvious to anyone viewing the tape that these young men were involved in criminal behavior, yet a man with a religious prefix to his name was there to support them, minimize what they had done, and accuse school officials and the local police of racism. On a lesser scale, I have also seen this type of situation in my community. One black reader of our local newspaper wrote in to protest the printing of pictures of people that had been arrested or were wanted by the police for various crimes because "all you ever print are black people - do you have a racial agenda?" Obviously the paper prints the pictures - black, white, Hispanic, etc. - of the people involved or wanted for criminal activity, regardless of race. It's as if some members of the black community are hesitant to accept the facts of a situation and punishment for their own group either because they don't trust the police or officials in charge, or they

For Such A Time As This…

…We Are But Small Voices

fear that they will somehow be smeared with the same negative label.

This situation saddens me. I feel that those involved are in need of a healing from the same God that many of these people worship. Each of them has been created in His likeness and is loved by Him. They are not simply part of a group - each is an individual Child of God! Could this Group Identity situation really be a "generational curse" stemming from the history of this nation when blacks needed to stick together to survive because they were all lumped together into the same situation due to color and slavery? I would like to see a true "emancipation" of many African-Americans from the feeling that they are judged because of the misdeeds of others who share their skin tone. I also feel that until the condemnation of the African-American community comes down upon those who are committing the crimes, some blacks will continue to see a charge in the newspaper or a guilty verdict in a court room as racism, not criminal behavior. I would hope that should a member of my own family commit a crime, that I would continue to try to support and love the individual while still holding them accountable for the choices he/she made.

As I look at this issue, I feel we should look upon ourselves as members of a family, church, or close group, not a race. How can any of us defend bad behavior just because the accused person shares your culture or color? Regardless of who judges you and why, your identity and self-esteem should not suffer from the negative, misguided, perhaps even prejudicial opinions of others. You should be judged for who you are, your positive accomplishments or your negative actions. This type of earthly situation would, I think, be a preview of Heaven because one day a Holy God will do just that!

Voice I: While I agree with many of the statements that Sue has made, I still feel that affirmative action is necessary. We as a race didn't have the head start that some of our white counterparts had. From the very beginning of our country, it was the whites who were the landowners and heads of financial institutions. Blacks initially had very little, and today we are still left behind. I feel that affirmative action has helped to bridge the gap, and has allowed us to make some awesome gains in the last several generations. Some people have truly moved from Harlem into the "Huxtable" lifestyle. However, many of our people are still plagued with the Harlem experience of poverty, drugs, government assistance, and black-on-black crime.

Whites made it a crime for slaves to learn to read, viewing this crime as serious enough to earn the death penalty. Now America is surprised when a majority of blacks consistently score in the lower percentiles of standardized tests. When I taught in a remediation program for over five years, I observed that the majority of our students were black. I believe that this situation does indeed go back to our history when we were not allowed to read.

Many reading these words will feel that I have gone out too far on a tangent. Yet I feel strongly that if you want to understand a present problem, look at the root or history behind it. It is hard for white America to accept the premise that current educational problems affecting black students could actually have stemmed from past injustices. Some people will say:

> "Get over slavery - I didn't enslave you."
> "Forget Jim Crow because things are equal now."
> "You can't use the 'white man is keeping me down' as an excuse any more because affirmative action has made everyone equal now."
> "Blacks have jobs whites can't even get, so get over it!"

To these statements I simply ask how can we get over it when less than five years ago a black man was dragged to death through the streets of Jasper, Texas, and more and more racial profiling has been exposed? Blacks have been and continue to be the target of many injustices because of the past. Jim Crow laws in the South used to prohibit any black man from looking directly at or even walking on the same side of the street as a white woman. Fourteen-year-old Emmett Till was brutally murdered for just whistling at a white woman - it cost him his life! Presently, many black men are still losing their lives of freedom because the jails continue to be filled with 80% black males. It seems like once lynching was made illegal, the prisons became the new lynching system for the hated and feared black man.

Over the last five years, more and more racial profiling has been exposed. Because of recent DNA advances, black men convicted of murder, rape, or other crimes have been cleared of their guilty verdicts and freed from prison. Once these men get out of prison, affirmative action laws can work in their favor to help them get an education, secure jobs, and have a better chance at success.

All of these examples relate to the history of African-Americans in this country. History is the past defining the present and perhaps the future. If history is responsible for the Magna Carta, and rights such as having trial by jury and protection of personal property, then why can't history also be responsible for the absence of black role models in the African-American community? Even in life, the laws of nature pretty much dictate that if I start behind, then there's a real strong chance that I will remain behind unless someday something strong, dramatic, or profound is added to put me equal or at a close second - forget "ahead." Even with such African-American high-profile success stories like Colin Powell, Condoleeza Rice, or Benjamin S. Carson, M. D., for the black community as a whole that someday has yet to happen.

Group Identity

Sue has noticed and commented that I often refer to African-American people involved in negative incidents as "we." I say that because blacks overall are seen by many as a bad race, just as the color black has often been seen as bad, evil, and disgusting. All you have to do is think about a few negative connotations associated with this color, such as: black lie, black magic, "black balling" someone, blacklist, and a black cat. They all historically symbolize the worst or most evil of all. As a black woman, when I see a black person involved in a negative situation - robbing or killing for little to no gain, or killing each other in street violence over a girl, a pair of shoes, or macho behavior - I feel a sense of failure also. I think, "Look at my people, falling into the same old negative stereotype." I have often said when I hear news reports of a petty crime, "I hope they aren't black." I feel that I am being judged as well because many people judge our race as one. The race as a whole started off low; most were slaves together and likewise, freed together. Even today, I strongly believe, the race will either rise or fall together.

Historically, if you were ¼ black, society considered you black. Today, the misdeeds, criminal and negative behavior of 20% - 25% of African-Americans color the image of the entire race. It is still hard for us to see ourselves as individuals when we are constantly being reminded of the effects of the past as a whole. In school, students will confront mixed-race peers with the question, "Are you black or white?" Because of preconceived notions, they want to know how to treat this person, based on who they say they are. Halle Berry's white mom is said to have told her daughter, "I am raising you as a black woman because society will make you choose, and treat you as one."

As long as I have to continue to search for the black faces in whatever is good, right, pure, and the best but seemingly find too few there, I will be disappointed. I have no problem finding them in the newspaper articles, the tabloids, and the crime statistics. As long as that continues, I will be a part of the group known as "we" rooting for "us" to make it.

Two **Voices As One:** Perspective is everything! We can't live another person's life; we can only speak from what we know and have experienced. Understanding and compassion come from communication and close inner action. Deidre and I had to be willing to trust each other enough to reveal our true feelings and open-minded enough to share personal ideas and experiences that helped us both grow. There is no one right answer. Equality truly lies in the "eyes of the beholder." However, in God's eyes, we are all equal and we are all loved!

Deidre B. Hester
Sue E. Whited

Chapter VIII - Must We Repeat History?

"Those who do not learn from the past, are destined to repeat it."
                        - George Santayana

Voice I: Through the years, I have gone out to minister in various correctional facilities, and I even helped pioneer the first Marine Institute on Virginia's peninsula. This was a program that used nautical concepts and knowledge, along with marine life, in a final attempt to catch troubled and delinquent youth before they were put through the criminal justice system. Needless to say, at both types of facilities, the majority of the faces were male. I can't even begin to count the number of times I left a jail cell feeling such emptiness, sadness, and depression because the majority of the male faces I saw there were black like mine. "Black like mine" echoed in the far recesses of my mind, and it never left. I often asked myself "why." I even asked God "why." His revelation came to me from the greatest and wisest book ever written - the Bible. Even though many great psychiatrists have stated that the way to solve a problem is to search for its roots, the Bible taught this concept even earlier: "Ye shall know the truth, and the truth shall make you free" (John 8:32). The Bible is our greatest resource and reveals to us that our past can influence our present and our future. As I studied these words, God revealed to me the answer to my question.

The history of black men in our country involves one of much shame, defeat, separation from home and family, as well as antagonizing and ridicule by many of the majority white males. I was shown that the result of this treatment and other factors over the years have left many black men torn down and unlikely to become assets in our society. In reality, I see a large number of black men being a liability. Not only are they liabilities in prisons, but are being seen as such on the street corner - hanging out, selling drugs, and leaving yet another legacy of wasted lives.

When I asked where are our forefathers, our brothers, our daddies, and our sons when communities were being forged, developed, and founded, the answer came that our men were being brutalized, beaten, downtrodden, and bred like cattle from hen-house to hen-house. They were also scorned in open shame and hung out like pieces of meat, burned at the stake, and left out for all to see. Out of this past came fear, shame, anger, and hurt. While the majority of white men had many advantages, the majority of black men had little to nothing. When blacks did try to achieve, they were sometimes brutally reminded to "stay in their place." The past definitely influenced the future as described in

Exodus 20:5: "Punishment for the sins of the fathers shall be visited on the child to the third and fourth generations," meaning negative attitudes, low self-esteem, and apathy, like sin, are perpetual and have been passed down from the father to the son. While many blacks overcame obstacles, remained strong and proud, becoming as successful as possible for their time and circumstances, others continued the negative attitudes that would hurt the black community. Like mold on bread, the spoil ruins the fresh, or one bad apple spreads its rot to the whole bushel.

Thank God for the kind white people He positioned to risk their own lives and families to treat blacks as equal and decent human beings. They gave some of our people land, homes, and hope. This hope was given to an otherwise doomed people. Even with these unselfish acts of kindness by some whites, the majority of black men would still live on to perpetuate separation, despair, and defeat within the walls of the black communities. Additionally, like every race of people, we have lost a portion of our men to homosexuality, interracial marriages, and prison. For the black community, these latter things have proven detrimental to our security and growth. With so many of the black men dead, despondent, or defeated, the black women were left to rear the children who would become the next generation.

My experience has shown me that a majority of discipline problems in the schools in my area have truly been with young, black males. Why? I feel it is because in public schools, you have a majority of black and white women trying to teach and discipline our black males, and this is a very difficult task. As I mentioned earlier (Ch. III - Teacher to Parent), it takes a man to make a man, as well as consistently maintain behavior in the classroom. These boys only respect power, viewing power from a male perspective, and may not initially respect a female teacher. While some female teachers succeed in this situation, many women have an uphill battle to gain respect from certain black males, and chaos in the classroom can result. Many black male students have been reared in homes where Mom is the only working adult. Our black community also contains many successful two-parent families, but I am focusing on those situations that continue to breed poverty, educational failure, and the defeated mind-set that says, "I need my check from the government to survive."

Many of our black youth see the only way out of poverty as sports, rap music, or drugs. Why is it when I asked a group of fourth grade students what their future goals were, all of the black boys told me they wanted to go into the NBA or NFL? Why didn't the ideas of medicine, law, scientific research, or the military enter their minds? Likewise, when I substituted for a group of high school students, all of the black males came into the room in a disruptive manner, gravitated to the back of the room, started playing cards, and refused to participate in the day's assignment. They refused to see school as relevant and the key to their future. While these two groups might represent only a small portion of students out there, they show that this way of thinking still exists and will continue to affect many on a wide scale. We must work to change these mind-sets, because

I believe overall that the black community still does not see ourselves as college graduates, business owners, or financially free. This is the legacy of the past, and it must end now because negative thinking has hurt us overall.

I believe now more than ever, that all people hurting over past and present injustices need to allow God to heal and change their hearts and minds. Once, when I was sharing my negative feelings about the "white man's" role in the destruction of the black community, a friend sharply reminded me how God had nailed all excuses to the cross. She went on to say that blacks as well as all other races of people must choose to rise above hate, prejudices, and injustices by emphatically stating, "Either you believe God's word or you don't!" This friend was Pastor Butler, another lifeline of mine. This conversation reminded me that Sue had also told me about Reggie White, the famous former NFL player; speaking similar words in a recent book (see Ch. VII). I thought about all of this and came to the conclusion that since I am a child of God, I had to believe that she and Reggie White were absolutely right. Just like Sue, Pastor Butler provided more healing to my wounds. Still I pondered, "Then how do we help the non-believers or people with no hope, no purpose or knowledge of God's plan for their lives to overcome and change their negative mind-sets?" I believe that these people can only benefit from our prayers for them and our lifestyles before them as children of the Light. Those of us who believe in God are His mouth-pieces and truly are the small voices of people in the middle (see Ch. XII) who will continue to make a positive difference to others around us. We can effectively do this by becoming our best for service to others first and ourselves last.

Conclusively, I have chosen to believe that because God delivered the Jews, the slaves, and the Gentiles, that He can deliver us all.

Voice II: I grew up during the Civil Rights movement. During my junior high years, Martin L. King, Jr. was marching, and students were staging sit-ins and riding interstate buses into the dangerous South to register blacks to vote. I remember being absolutely infuriated when George Wallace stood blocking the doorway to the University of Alabama to the entrance of black students. In West Virginia I knew very few black people, but even at that young age, I realized that what was happening before the television cameras (and before Forrest Gump memorialized it in theaters) was very, very wrong. I wrote Gov. Wallace a letter in bright, red ink for emphasis, and told him, "you are a red neck who embarrasses people like me who look like you!" Then I felt that I done my part for the Civil Rights Movement.

During my years as an Air Force wife, I would occasionally meet spouses who represented different racial groups, but I never became friends with any of them, nor invited them to our home. However, I do remember an experience in Biloxi, Mississippi, when our oldest son entered the second grade at Jefferson Davis Elementary School. Picking him up after his first day at this new school, my husband and I were eager to hear all the details of his experiences. The one thing that seemed to interest Ric the most, but also appeared to cause him some concern, was the fact that his new teacher, Mrs. Nixon, was black. She had seemed exceptionally sweet and understanding when I dropped him off that morning, but now Dad was going into the school in uniform to pick up our son. As Ric climbed into our van, he nervously turned to his father and asked, "Did you see my teacher - she's black, you know." Richard and I grinned, thinking this was certainly an obvious observation. However, looking back I realize that since our family had not had any close interactions with black people before, Ric had no experience with them. I'm glad his first such relationship was with a positive, caring, and professional woman. I'm also thankful that Dad didn't disappoint our son by having a negative reaction to this new learning environment. Imagine the difference it would have made if he had not accepted a black teacher for his son or had made comments criticizing her race. This is how it all starts and racial discrimination infects another generation.

Must we repeat history, or can we as American citizens agree that the past is gone, and that we will learn from it and move on. If not, the result may be similar to that occurring elsewhere around the world. Arabs and Jews call the same patriarch "Father" because Abraham sired both Ishmael and Isaac. His descendants are now warring with each other, causing death and destruction in the Middle East. In Northern Ireland, Catholics and Protestants have a long history of religious bigotry and bloodshed. In Africa, tribal warfare has caused massacres of hundreds of thousands of people. Let us learn that this type of behavior is the bitter fruit of hatred and discrimination. America should be better than that because it was founded on Judeo/Christian principles. We could become the country that is described on the base of the Statue of Liberty * if only we decide to look Above for the answer. Every generation has its defining moment. I hope this is ours - that we look to the One who created us all and realize that we are all children of the same Heavenly Father. One of His greatest commandments asks us to love others as we love ourselves. Will we finally get it right? I hope so.

    * "Give me your tired, your poor,
Your huddled masses yearning to breathe free,
The wretched refuse of your teaming shore
Send these, the homeless, tempest-tossed to me
I lift my lamp beside the golden door."
- Emma Lazarus

Two Voices As One: It is time for the past to be put to rest, especially in the areas mentioned in this chapter. Personal perspective can be a powerful thing, for when a person has had one negative experience after another, he/she sometimes feels that his/her life will never change. As teachers, we are all about change and the transformation that education can bring into a person's life. History that is shameful and wrong never needs to be repeated. It is our hope that this chapter will help at least one person decide that the future is the place to reside. Preparing for and looking to the future gives all of us hope that tomorrow will be much better than today.

Deidre B. Hester
Sue E. Whited

For Such A Time As This…
…We Are But Small Voices

Chapter IX - The Reality of Race: Operation Oreo

"If you can learn a simple trick, Scout, you'll get along a lot better with all kinds of folks. You never really understand a person until you consider things from his point of view… until you climb into his skin and walk around in it."
- *TO KILL A MOCKINGBIRD*
by Harper Lee

Deidre B. Hester
Sue E. Whited

Voice II: Our urban area of Hampton, Virginia, is culturally and ethnically diverse, and this diversity is represented in the schools as well. My sixth and eighth grade classroom might contain a 40-45% Caucasian, 40-45% African-American, and 10-20% mix of Asian, Hispanic, and mixed-race students. This "melting pot" makes for a wonderfully eclectic academic atmosphere, but could also cause negative clashes and misunderstandings at times. One of the points I tried to emphasize in as many ways as I could was that you cannot judge a person based on their "earth suit," their skin color; that the way a person looked was not a determinate of what kind of person they were. I tried to teach my students that what mattered most was the kind of person they were on the inside - that their character, their soul was much more important. My friendship with Mrs. Hester was evident to all our students, and occasionally we would team-teach on a topic or project of interest to us both. One of the most unique of these projects would come to be known as "Operation Oreo."

Part of the opening each day in my social studies classes is to have a discussion on current events - the news. For a long time this particular year, one of the leading stories concerned the O.J. Simpson murder trial. I tried not to dwell on this brutal case, but would relate important developments as they occurred. Finally the verdict was about to be announced and was scheduled for 1:00 p.m. on a weekday when the third period class would be in my room. Since I had a television set - affectionately called "Big Bertha" - attached to cable and permanently set up in a corner of my room, several adults also found their way into my class that day so they could hear the verdict also. Everyone was quiet as Judge Ito read the jury's verdict: "not guilty." Almost immediately the room became loud with cheers and clapping, and as I looked toward the noise, I was struck with a sight I will never forget. Most of my black students were joyously expressing their pleasure with the verdict, while many of my white students were incredulously looking on in amazement, their mouths dropping open. The principal and assistant principal looked on with me, and we all remarked later on the racial divide that was so evident in my room that day. I couldn't put that picture out of my mind. How could the same group of students hear the same news reports, analyze the same data, and be so overwhelmingly divided as to the fairness or rightness of the verdict? I came to the conclusion that it was all a matter of cultural perspective. The black students felt that O.J. got a fair trial, and that he was acquitted because no one proved he had committed the crime. Finally, the "black man" had gotten justice and fair treatment in a court of law. The white students seemed to feel the exact opposite, that the trial had proven this man guilty beyond a reasonable doubt and that there had not been justice, but injustice done that day by the jury.

The next day when I walked another class to the cafeteria for lunch, I once again noticed a phenomenon that had interested me earlier in the school year, but "screamed out" at me this day. Upon looking around the crowded cafeteria, it was obvious that racial segregation was occurring. Not the illegal kind, but a self-imposed preferential kind. The students were almost entirely sitting with people who looked like them. Black students were sitting together, as were white ones. The Asian, Hispanic, and other students had also chosen to eat with and talk to those of their own ethnic background as much as possible. I decided to try an experiment to bridge this cultural divide within not only this class, but all my other classes as well.

I described the scenario I had witnessed to my third period class the next day, and asked them questions about each other. Did Tommy know where Makalia had gone to elementary school? Did Jamal know whether Billy or Susan had any brothers? What was Angela's favorite food? When the lack of answers proved puzzling to the class, I announced a week-long experiment. These students were to regroup themselves during lunch, and sit beside someone from their class that they did not really know, someone who did not look like them. During their lunch time that next week, they were to share personal information about themselves with this classmate and get to know one another in a new and more intimate way.

When I went to the cafeteria on the first day of "Oreo" week, there they were, regrouped and talking away! When they saw me, they waved, wanting me to see that they were doing what I had asked. By Wednesday, these new groups were interacting as if they had been doing this for a long time. I walked over to the tables and the groups got even more noisy. I told them that I was proud of them and asked how it was going. They started chanting, "Oreo, Oreo," and began putting their hands in the middle of the table, alternating colors - one white hand, one black hand, etc. The principal saw and heard all the commotion at the table and because several of the larger students were bent over the middle of the table to stretch in their hand, she was concerned that something serious was happening. When I explained to her what we were doing, she and I reached in and put our hands in an appropriate spot. We were honorary members of the Oreo Society. Both of us felt that this was a dynamic moment. How different from the previous week when students were not united, but divided by perceived differences.

Later, when we discussed what the students had learned during this experiment, what I had hoped would happen had indeed occurred. Students learned that they were much more alike than different. Little brothers were a pain, regardless of whether they were black, white, Asian, or Hispanic. Everyone was interested in music, clothes, movies, makeup, etc. They were all teenagers and had lot of things in common, but they had never taken the time to really get to know people who looked differently than they did on the outside. We took that topic to a world view, and decided that people in South America, Africa, Asia, Europe, and Australia would probably have some of the same similarities that Americans do. Eighth graders were able to come to the conclusion that our most important similarity is our humanity - we are all more alike than we are different. What a blessing to see that what I had innately felt all my life and learned personally from my friendship with Deidre had been multiplied into many more lives.

Voice I: Like Sue, I noticed the racial divide, but unlike the response she had, which was to find a way to teach or incorporate a life lesson, I needed to internalize it more - analyze why it was so. I thought and pondered over what I had seen and heard repeated about O.J., until I just stopped watching everything about the case on TV. This was a month prior to the verdict, and I began asking myself and God, "Who else would have wanted Nicole dead?" Each day I prayed that God would allow this vicious killer to be found. What person would commit such a hideous, unspeakable crime, and take a mommy from her precious babies? Who would do such a thing? My mind continued to come to the same conclusion - it had to be O.J.! He probably did it or had someone else do it. When an answer from God didn't seem to come, my mind still told me, "the Juice did it!"

It amazed me that I didn't feel angry that this man I thought was guilty had been set free from this terrible crime. Honestly, a part of me felt relieved or justified. I further rationalized that a lot of blacks probably felt that O.J. was guilty, but for once a black man had enough money and enough reputation to buy his freedom. White people had done this for years. The wicked spirit of buying indulgences (a Catholic term which meant paying for sins) was now affecting a new race and era. Still another part of me was glad. Now white America could see how so many blacks felt when the guilty, smug murderers of Emmett Till were declared not guilty, or when four precious, innocent church girls were killed by the Klan in Birmingham, Alabama. I was so torn by my feelings because, in reality, this verdict had nothing to do with earlier times. I could only ask God to forgive me for how I felt. It was wrong for me to rationalize that what was done so long ago could justify why a part of me was satisfied that O.J. was found innocent. That was wrong, but I found that the truth sets us free.

That popular Bible verse caused me to remember when Martin L. King, Jr. said, "Free at last, free at last, thank God Almighty we're free at last!" Perhaps he meant that blacks were on their way to being treated like equal citizens in a country they had helped to build but weren't able to fully experience. They had been unable to partake of the benefits of a good education and the American dream due to discrimination. The Civil Rights movement had truly made the black community free at last because they could now enjoy privileges unprecedented in our country's history.

The freedom I desired went deeper, however, because I wanted to be free from all prejudices and past hates. I wanted to be able to speak my hurt as a black person and then get a response to begin my healing. With Sue I could do this. I was glad for Operation Oreo because it felt good to have someone just listen, and she did. Sue and I had always tried to demonstrate to our students that we went beyond the surface in our friendship. The way we shared, interacted, and taught the interdisciplinary lessons we did on the Civil Rights era proved this. We once even applied for a grant for a program we entitled, "You Can't Judge a Book By Its Cover," seeking to expand our lesson and reach even more young people. However, when it was denied, we concluded that if not on a wide scale, we would continue to teach it in our classrooms and affect the future in this smaller way. This message of learning to love, appreciate, or just recognize the differences would help those we taught to understand that we are still more alike than different. We all truly need to feel love and give love; feel appreciated and accepted to fulfill our purpose in this life.

I liked Sue's "Operation Oreo." Now what we had been doing all along had a cool name. She had experimented with what I call "selective segregation," where we choose to be with those who are most like us simply because we feel more comfortable or familiar with those people. I totally agree with Sue - all people are more alike than different, but we do have different cultures. People with similar cultures have a unique bond, and because there are those differences, we should seek to learn about and appreciate them. I believe the differences give us more spice in life.

It is just like the Bible said, "There is nothing new under the sun." In the 1960's another teacher, Jane Elliott, used differences in eye color to teach the concept of unwarranted discrimination to a group of elementary students through an experiment called the "Blue Eye/Brown Eye Exercise." A decade later in the 1970s, Coach Boone and Coach Yoast endured a similar situation in the Gettysburg College experience made popular in Disney's "Remember the Titans," starring Denzel Washington and Will Pattan. Even before the movie's release, and twenty years later, Sue - in the early 1990s was inspired by God to bring about racial unity as had numerous unknown and unsung reformers before her. Each of these teachers were fighting the same battle: the age-old, demonic spirit of racism. But maybe now society would be ready for a major healing among the races. Since everything comes line upon line and precept upon precept, maybe now society could handle change within the races on a larger scale. Maybe Operation Oreo would catch on like the "Blue Eye/Brown Eye Exercise" concept to demonstrate that discrimination is very hurtful and wrong. Maybe, just maybe, Operation Oreo could be offered in other schools' extra-curricular or after school programs. Maybe Operation Oreo could be taken across the city, state, or nation by way of our classrooms, colleges, churches, and workplaces. Maybe, perhaps maybe, Operation Oreo could be the main platform upon which people of every race could begin to talk, learn about differences, agree to disagree, work out hard feelings, and grow as human beings. Perhaps, maybe …?

Two **Voices As One:** So many black people don't know how white people think, and white people don't understand the exuberance and feelings of blacks. Hispanics, Latinos, Asian groups, and others need to be included in this Operation Oreo mix because we have discovered that "black and white" is only the beginning. Other racial groups have faced similar discrimination and should be included if the healing process is to be effective. Understanding only comes from spending time with someone who is different from you. Until you get to know someone for real - get inside their "skin" - you will never bridge the gap between the races because you won't really know who the person is. Take a leap of faith and try it; you could be incredibly blessed as a result!

Chapter X - "Acting White"… An Inside Story of Academic Underachievement

"Today parents and educators must combat the perverse view among many black kids that serious scholarship is <u>a white thing</u>."

> \- University of California professor John Ogbu *

Voice II: I was always a good student. I tried hard and worked to fix what I perceived was lacking in my academic life. When I attended college to become a teacher, I had no idea that many of my future students wouldn't approach their studies in a like manner. Regardless of race or gender, many students today seem to lack the inner work ethic or willingness to do well in school. This is why educators, administrators, and school systems are continually coming up with external motivators like pizza parties, gift certificates, and honor roll celebrations to encourage students to work harder and perform better. This lack of student motivation really surprised me when I entered the classroom as a new teacher. I felt that if I did my job to present the material in an interesting and stimulating way, the students would be encouraged and want to learn.

Over the years my idealism has faded somewhat and I have learned that this doesn't always happen with many students whose main interests are their sports activities and social life. For them school is only a place to see and be seen. In their book, No Excuses:

Closing the Racial Gap in Learning, Abigail and Stephen Thernstrom* * point out that nearly 25% of all students leave high school with academic skills that are "Below Basic." This means that the NAEP (National Assessment of Educational Progress) rates them as unable to show even a partial mastery of knowledge and skills that are necessary for passing work at their grade level. If you look at one individual category, African-American students, the picture gets even worse. Forty percent of the black students score below basic in writing, 70% do so in math, science results are 75% lower than basic, with history and geography test scores no better. This means that employers of many black high school graduates are actually hiring people who perform just a little better than eighth graders in both reading and U. S. history, and even worse in math and geography. Regardless of the category, the unending challenge remains: how do you awaken the clueless clients, our students, to the necessity of using their time wisely to prepare themselves for high school and their futures?

Every year throughout my years of teaching, I have continually sought to encourage students to do their best, not only in sports, the arts, or other interests, but also in the classroom. I try to show them through stimulating quotes, newspaper articles, and the examples of others that hard work in school really pays off later when they are accepted into college, a university, or training programs that will allow them to live a good life and be of help to others. However, I never expected to encounter a baffling, infuriating mind-set held by some African-American students which they called "acting white."

I first discovered this situation while teaching eighth graders several years after I began my teaching career. A very attractive black student came to me in tears over comments that had been made to her in the hall of our school. She said that some of the other popular black girls in her group had told her that if she made the Honor Roll again, they would drop her from their group because they had no respect for their people who "acted white." When I asked her what they meant, she shook her head and told me, "I'm still trying to figure it out." Never one to stop when there's a question to be answered, I plunged into this confusing situation and was dumbfounded by the responses I heard. It seemed that succeeding in school was seen by a number of black students as a "white" thing to do. They saw the black role in school to be sports, music, dancing, and the social scene. Where they excelled naturally and easily, they ruled. However, in the classroom, where good grades required a lot more work and effort, it was easier to dismiss this challenging area as the domain of white students. While "white men can't jump," they could learn math formulas, and where white girls "had no rhythm," they could test better than the black dance queens. I tried to counter this type of thinking with the idea that there was once a time when Michael Jordan had never touched a basketball and had no idea how to dunk. It took a lot of work, practice, and will-power for #23 to achieve all that he did to become the top at his game, and Michael actually graduated with a BA degree from the University of North Carolina in 1986. Why couldn't my students decide to go for academics with the same work ethic?

Not all of my students grasped this type of thinking. However, a majority did understand the idea that many things do not come easily at first, but with hard work, determination, and the unwillingness to give up, improvement will definitely come. They could note the comparison or similarity with sports. Many of my students remembered when they began to play football, basketball, hockey, soccer, or began cheering. The moves, plays, and confidence weren't there in the beginning, but steadily improved with practice and experience. Nothing pleases me more as a teacher than to see a student slowly but surely improve in my class. Moving from a "D" the first nine weeks to a "B" by the end of the year is a dramatic change and a true lesson in life. Hard work does pay off regardless of the area of involvement.

Whether my underachievers are black, white, Hispanic, Asian, or mixed-race and characterized as gifted, advanced, average, or low ability, this is a lesson that is so important to learn. I hope I have taught it as well as I have taught history. The old cliché is correct: "If at first you don't succeed - try, try again." I have added to it a quote from Verne Hill which states: "If you always do what you've always done, you'll always get what you always got." This aptly states that you have to change your method if you aren't satisfied with the results. Additionally, you have to understand that you are a person, an individual with gifts that require work to shine. Don't ever allow yourself to be characterized as a race or a group (see Ch. VII). You are responsible to yourself, your family, and to God - not your friends. One day they will go their way and you will go yours. Why would you allow them to define you today? Don't act black or white, grunge or hip-hop, just be "yourself" and try your best to develop what God gave you at birth. Your fingerprints are unique and so are you, so work hard to develop your special talents!

* Black American Students in an Affluent Suburb: A Study of Academic Disengagement

** Cited by Walter E. Williams, John M. Olin Professor of Economics at George Mason University in his editorial, "No excuses for students failing in school."

Voice I: I agree wholeheartedly with Sue. I have overhead students yell out phrases like: "She's acting white," when an African-American student chooses to use standard English and ignore commonly used slang such as "We be tired," or "She wear them clothes too much," and "He wants to be black" because a white classmate listens to rap music and wears the hip-hop clothing associated with the black culture. Several years ago, Sue shared with me the term "whigger" which meant "a white person who acts black." These students seemed to admire the music, clothing, and style of the black culture and easily adopted it as their own. Is it surprising then that some black students are seen by their peers as trying to act white when they choose and enjoy making good grades and give this a priority?

I believe that some black students associate making good grades more with the white culture because in their homes education wasn't held in high esteem as the parents were so busy just trying to make ends meet and provide for their families. Traditionally within the black culture, more homes were parented by single working moms who struggled to pay bills and put food on the table with little time for reading stories and teaching about colors and shapes to their preschool children. Statistics show that this problem still occurs today because the majority of children needing Head Start services throughout our country continue to be among the minority races. Many of these parents consistently put more emphasis on sports, shoes, name brand clothing, and music over books and education because, I believe, they view these things as the ticket out of poverty and into the good life. Why else is it that I have seen so many black students come to school with expensive name brand clothing and shoes, but without their homework or even their textbooks. Moreover, parents scramble to put their sons in recreational sports programs at younger and younger ages, but show little to no support for school programs, such as PTA meetings, back-to-school nights, or teacher conferences. It will be difficult to change these mind-sets as long as people can see sports figures and musical stars making millions of dollars more than doctors, lawyers, accountants, and engineers. As I have mentioned before, many little black boys dream of the NFL and NBA (see Ch. VIII) and see themselves as future stars there. As a matter of fact, years ago Sue taught one eighth grader who made his dream come true in the NBA.

When I first came to Davis Middle School, I remember Sue talking about this student she had taught the previous year who was so talented athletically and artistically. She was concerned because he had so many problems in his life, and wasn't doing well academically. The promise was there, but would it be fulfilled? She continued to attend his games, write him notes of encouragement, send him McDonald's coupons, and even drop by his high school to see him before important play-off games. She wanted me to speak to him because we shared the one thing that they didn't - our race. When I met him one day, I told Sue that he was a good looking kid as she had told me, but I felt that he was too cocky to listen to me at the time. Perhaps years later the day would come when he would realize and appreciate what she was trying to do for him. Today, #3 on the 76ers has made his millions in the arena of basketball, but I wonder if Allen Iverson realizes that his eighth grade social studies teacher still thinks about him, prays for him, and wishes him success in life, not just on the basketball court. He made it, but very few little boys do. That is why it is so important that they learn that education - not sports - is the key to their futures.

"It's a Black thing, you wouldn't understand" is just as much an obsolete phrase as "She's acting white" and "He's acting black" should be. If a person enjoys the culture of another race - that's a good thing. If we have freedom of speech in this country, we should definitely have freedom of choice without condemnation and ridicule by others. Education is the key to a better way of life. It always has been and it always will be. Take advantage of public education through high school and look for opportunities to fund your way through higher education by scholarships, grants, and loans. While it's good to have other dreams and goals, they aren't always fulfilled. However, education will never let you down!

Two **Voices As One:** Over the years there have been times when we have seen students doing much less than we know they could do. They allow peers to negatively influence their education without realizing the lifelong impact it will have. They are willing to get up early and wait in line at the mall for the latest sports star's tennis shoe, but they rarely have the same motivation for their academic life. Somehow we have to make both students and parents understand that the same energy and involvement young people invest in sports, music, and shopping for clothes has to find its way into the classroom experience as well.

For Such A Time As This…
…We Are But Small Voices

The United Negro College Fund's motto is "A mind is a terrible thing to waste."

We agree - why would you even consider it?

Deidre B. Hester
Sue E. Whited

Chapter XI - Shame on You

"There is a way that seems right to a man, but in the end it leads to death."

- Proverbs 14:12

Voice II: I am writing this chapter after viewing news clips yesterday of the latest MTV award show which among other things broadcast an "open mouth" kiss between three women. This is just the latest example of the wasteland of television programming that is available to the American public, both young and old. On prime time programming today you can view sexual situations, hear profanity and God's name taken in vain repeatedly, see young people totally disrespect their parents in family sitcoms, watch shocking, disgusting events on reality shows, and ogle gyrating, partially-clad females in music videos while the male singer/rapper uses derogatory names for them right in their presence.* Some cultural experts say this is one reason why our country is reviled in fundamentalist countries in the Middle East and other places around the world. They view our movies and television programs, and judge all Americans by what they see. Did the decadence on the small and large screens lead to 9-11? You be the judge. The more troubling observation might be that regardless of which countries see us as the Great Satan or an infidel nation due to perceived immorality, our children are growing up accepting what they see and hear on television and the movies as appropriate behavior that they want to copy.

Over the last thirty to forty years, movies have become much more violent and sexually explicit. In order to receive an "R" rating which means a bigger cross-over audience and more profits, movie producers make sure there are several bedroom scenes or profanity-laden dialogue or over-the-top graphic violence. Some movies showcase all of these in a visual smorgasbord of smut. Like the proverbial frog, we have been slowly but surely "cooked to death" by the ever-increasing level of the things we formerly wouldn't have accepted, but now have seen so much of that we don't even think to protest. However, television and movies are only the beginning of the negative influences affecting our children.

Have you tried to buy attractive but suitable and age-appropriate clothing for girls lately? I don't know who is designing outfits for young ladies in this new millennium, but I think they are stuck with the "Lolita look" even in elementary school. Bared midriffs, low-riding jeans, thongs, tee-strapped tops, stretchy body-clinging outfits, and shorts so short that they are probably a health hazard! It doesn't take much detective work to deduce that these types of clothing that hang from the racks in most department and discount stores are based on designs worn by the pop music divas. When the eight to thirteen-year-old Britney, Christina, and Kim "wanna bees" walk the halls of their schools, they end up looking totally out of place and downright promiscuous. Maybe that's why some of our male students have trouble concentrating in school! I have to question why more parents don't refuse to buy these clothes. The excuse that "everybody's wearing it," or "I won't fit in" just doesn't work for me. These are your daughters - why would you send them out in public looking like street walkers?

If pop music styles affect the way the girls dress, you only have to look on the other side of the hall to see a similar problem with the male wardrobe. The hip hop craze caught on years ago, with baggy pants, multi-layered clothing, gang-suggesting bandanas, "bling-bling" jewelry, and a "rolling" stroll complete with constantly gyrating arms. School has become a place to showcase how well you can

>154

copy the latest fad from the world of music videos, not a place to do well academically.

Speaking of music, young people have always loved music, and so do I. But if I turn on the cable music channels, the images ruin my appreciation for the tune or rhythm. Then when I decipher the lyrics on some songs, I just get angry. There seems to be no boundaries as to what is said or sung. I teach Social studies, so I am familiar with the freedom of speech argument. The Ku Klux Klan used it for years as they spewed their garbage to the public. When people stopped listening, their influence started to die. In the case of the musical refuse, I just keep thinking that my students, my Godchildren, and other young people might be listening to these words, and if so, their minds are being filled with images that are not good for them. People might say who am I to judge the creativity of another? I would answer that I am an adult who recognizes obscenity when it occurs, either in images or words.

The computer, one of the most life-changing inventions for America and the world during the last generation, has become an area of danger for our young people, and indeed, everyone. Pornography is readily available in our living rooms, family rooms, or even our teenagers' bedrooms because there are estimated to be seven million X-rated Web sites available on line. Advertisements for these sites pop up on everyone's e-mail addresses giving anyone who is interested, any kind of filth or perversion they might desire. Not just bestiality or bondage, but child porn. These types of shocking pictures rob our children of what little innocence they might possess at younger and younger ages. We are living in an age of spiritual darkness and desperately need more people to step up and shed some light for those who are lost by fighting against these types of web sites.

This leads me back to the title of this chapter. Shame on you pop, rap, hip hop and other musical stars who are leading America's young people astray and pocketing millions of dollars by doing so! I know - my generation had Elvis and the Beatles who were shocking in their day - but did you ever see them star in the type of music videos shown on MTV and BET any hour of the day? Even 70s rock star,

Alice Cooper, thinks some of today's pop stars have gone too far, "You really don't want to see Britney Spears to be naked on stage," he says. "You want her to tease you, but you don't want to see her naked." The very fact that the recent awards show had to resort to a demonstration of lesbian kisses during a musical number for shock value shows just how far down the ladder of decadence we have come. Any thinking American knows that type of act would never have gotten out of the strip joints or peep shows a few years ago.

When does it stop? How far will it go? Why shouldn't a holy God be ready to destroy us as He did Sodom and Gomorrah for their unceasing immorality? These are serious questions for serious times, but the underlying reason for my questions remains. How can any of these things I have mentioned have a positive effect on our children and young people? They are becoming hardened to all manner of things that are offensive to many of us, wanting even more violence, sexuality, profanity, carnality, and gore. Everyone who has contributed to this immoral entertainment industry will one day be held accountable.

As for now, it's time for adults who care to begin to speak out, petition our elected leaders, and stop allowing the liberal media, press, and organizations to continue to push the envelope on what we will legally allow in this country (see Ch. XII). Parents, get serious about doing your job as a mom or dad, and realize that sometimes you have to draw the line on what you will accept in your children's lives because their futures are at stake! Remember, regardless of their ages, your sons and daughters will always be your children. They will grow up and make choices based on what they saw, heard, and learned under your roof. I hope they make you proud!

Voice I: "Who let the dogs out?" "Back that thing up…" "I like big butts…" "It's getting hot in here, so take off all your clothes"

These are not the familiar lyrics that I want to hear playing in my teenager's room. Yet, some in society see these as fun and funny tunes, even using them on TV and radio as messages to promote an interesting way of life. I am so ashamed at how many of the videos offered on TV allow our youth to dress in such provocative and disgusting clothing. Some even fall into the false perception that certain groups of people are sex-crazed and sex-driven freaks. These videos send the message that all these types of people can do is party, drive lavishly expensive cars, make babies, and play ball. Aside from being ashamed, I'm angry, and the objects of my anger are those in the black community who have allowed my race to be stereotyped in this way.

So I turn off the TV and go to the mall to enjoy a shopping experience with my daughter. It is a sad day when all I could find in popular department stores are low-cut tops and tight, hip-hugger pants to buy her for back to school. Many clothes I saw in the stores seemed to scream, "Here it is - come and get it!" Wake up people - put down your basketballs and pick up a good book! Bump and grind and shaking your "booty" should not be the theme of your life because you have far more talents than that. As you read and learn about history, you will discover how many African-Americans, as well as people from other ethnic groups, come from a fine legacy of doctors, lawyers, inventors, and military heroes. You could join that list of outstanding Americans if only you cared about your future as much as you do about the latest songs, fashions, and dances.

If any group of people wants to change how they are viewed by society, they are the ones who must play a major role in that transformation. It is time for us to make things happen for ourselves. We must use the human resources that God places in our lives. Don't look at the package or the color in which it comes; just look for your lifelines because they are out there. All you need is to just find one, and I know you have them because God put them there. People of all color are told by God in His word that "we are the lenders and not the borrowers," "the head and not the tail," and "above and not beneath" (Deut. 28:12-13). Seek to serve your fellow man first, and your needs will be met naturally because it's God's law and it works.

I want to challenge everyone to work hard and bring society to what should be our best music in life. Instead of "dogs," "butts," and "heat," those popular lyrics that drag us down to our base levels, the most pressing concern should be those things that elevate us as a people, not degrade us as a group. As long as we allow anything, our nation will continue to fall. Remember, Rome was destroyed from within by its immorality. Will America follow suit? As one familiar and wise cliché states, "You have to stand for something, or you will fall for anything!" In my opinion, our country is falling rapidly because too few people are willing to speak out against anything. Galatians 6:9-10 encourages us to stand strong saying,

"Let us not be weary in doing good; for at the proper time, we will reap a harvest if we do not give up. Therefore, as we have opportunity, let us do good."

This should be the tune and theme of our lives: united we must stand for righteousness or divided we will fall. One of my favorite Winan songs sums it up perfectly:

Deidre B. Hester
Sue E. Whited

"I remember when life was so simple
You did or you didn't,
You would or you wouldn't
But it ain't like that anymore.

I remember when life was so easy
People said what they meant - they were either for it or against.
But it ain't like that anymore.
Somewhere we lost the score.

I remember when life was so simple
Boys grew into men,
Little girls to women then.
But it ain't like that anymore.

I remember when life was so easy
Parents were the light -
Through them we saw what was right.
But it ain't like that any more.

Somewhere we lost the score
Bring back the days of 'Yay and Nay'
When we could plainly see the way
When it was up to us to choose whether to win or lose.

Bring back the time when we could see
What it was we were to be,
Caught in the midst of complexity
We search for 'Yay and Nay.'

We knew where we belonged
What was right and what was wrong
Bring back the days . . . . . .

Bring Back the Days of 'Yay and Nay' - *The Winans*

162

Two **Voices As One:** Shame is sometimes a good thing when it results in changed behavior. Even though the media, department stores, and the computer make so many negative things available today, parents and guardians still have the final choice in what they allow. Our hope in this chapter is to awaken readers to the fact that what parents allow in their home in the form of television, videos, clothing, and behavior is reflected in their children. Teenagers may resent hearing, but do understand the phrase "Garbage in… garbage out." It's time for us as adults - the parents, teachers, leaders, and pastors - to dump the garbage in the can and leave it there so it doesn't affect the lives of the next generation. We have been told to "train up a child in the way he should go" (Proverbs 22:6), and not allow him to find his own way through trial and error or fall into the excuse that "everyone else is doing it.".

Too many children are raising themselves and too many parents are allowing it.

As this book goes to press, the FCC is investigating Super Bowl XXXVIII's half-time show where up to 100 million people witnessed split second nudity during a musical number. FCC's chief Michael Powell is quoted as saying, "I am outraged at what I saw. Like millions of Americans, my family and I gathered around the television for a celebration. Instead that celebration was tainted by a classless, crass, and deplorable stunt. Our nation's children, parents, and citizens deserve better."

"Preach the Word; be prepared in season and out of season; correct, rebuke, and encourage… For the time will come when men will not put up with sound doctrine. Instead, to suit their own desires, they will gather around them a great number of teachers to say what their itching ears want to hear. They will turn their ears away from the truth and turn aside to myths."

2 Timothy 4: 2 – 4

Chapter XII - People in the Middle

"Who knows but that you were placed here for such a time as this."

- Esther 4:14

Voice I: "The people in the middle" is a phrase that refers to those people who are concerned with accomplishing their God-ordained purpose in life. It is my opinion that these people are not concerned about race, denomination, or the special rights of any one particular group of people. The focus of PIMs (People in the Middle) is the well-being of others. This group realizes that we must invest in our youth today in order that they might become an asset tomorrow. They believe that children are one of our greatest human resources and that we need to prepare, preserve, and protect them as never before. PIMs are mindful of the examples we set before them as teachers, leaders, lay people, and parents, realizing that personal prejudices and immoral behavior can be carefully taught by one generation to another. PIMs can be found as the leaders of Boy Scouts, little league teams, after-school tutors, and dance instructors. No doubt the coach in the movie, "Sandlot," learned to be a PIM before it was all said and done!

PIMs know that all people are unique and different, but that our differences don't matter in the overall picture. We should be the "light of the world" and the "salt of the earth." We come from all walks of life, nationalities, and races. We are the ones from every area that look outside of ourselves to try to understand others. However, today there are those people who would try to persuade you to see others in a different, more negative way.

Louis Farrakhan was once quoted in a *Time* magazine issue as being the "voice of Black America." I was angered by this and vehemently told Sue that, "he does not speak for me!" As a well-known leader of American Muslims, he once called God's chosen people - the Jews - "the devil" and actively promotes dissension between the black and white races. Likewise, I'm sure, many white people have been ashamed of the rantings of David Duke and other white supremacists, or Middle Easterners of the evil terrorist acts of Osama bin Laden.

I say that the people in the middle are not like these individuals. They want to get along with and understand other races. PIMs have to speak out against racial inequalities and injustices. They feel that they must help our children to learn that we are all interconnected and what one group does can and has hurt others. For example, the jail systems in America may be overcrowded with a majority of black men, but every race of people helps maintain and pay for the upkeep of these "bad boys" of society. Likewise if more people are not interested or involved in our current public education system, the productivity of the students, those future tax-paying citizens, could affect their retirement funds.

It is time for those of us who really care for others to realize that we are our "brothers' keepers." It is time for us - the people in the middle - to rise and set aside racial, denominational, and cultural differences and see the greater work - to preserve, prepare, and propel our youth to succeed and not fail.

We must accept the realities of life and openly use what we know to solve our societal demons. We can no longer push them under the carpet with the old, worn-out excuses that "It's always been this way and won't ever change." The call to the occasion is now, and it is to the people in the middle, the ones who believe that they can make a difference right where they are for the bigger picture.

Here are some realities that, I believe, we need to face in order to move forward:

- Cultural differences do exist
- We must use the knowledge of these cultural differences to help improve our schools, work places, communities, and churches
- Not every child can or will go to college
- Each individual must be expected to contribute to society, not just receive from it
- We are in the 21st Century and our educational system must be also

People in the middle - I know you're out there in every community, city, and state. I want to encourage you to get involved somewhere, even if it's just in one place with one person. Remember, tomorrow may never come for you, so what better thing could you do today than to make a difference, right where you are?

Voice **II:** In our society today, those on the left and those on the right are often heard debating issues on news programs, talking to famous interviewers like Oprah Winfrey, Larry King, and Bill O'Reilly, and writing best-selling books. The majority of us will never be interviewed because we are somewhere in the middle of these opinions, and our voices are rarely heard on television or elsewhere. That is why Deidre decided to write this book and graciously asked me to participate with her so that the "still, small voices" of those in the middle could be heard.

Those of us who are working hard all week at jobs that support our families have little time left over to become involved in the dialogue over government, political candidates, new laws, educational reforms, religious liberty, and other varying types of issues. We are the ones who support this nation, taxed to the max and trying to make sense of all the talk from those supporting the conservative, independent, and liberal agendas. We are quietly coaching recreational teams for our children, taking to the mountains or the seashores for brief family vacations, and trying to instill our values and beliefs to our children through church, scouting, music lessons, and other activities. Life is very complicated and seems to be getting even more demanding than it was in the late 60s and early 70s when I began raising children. Voices are clamoring at us from every side, leaving very little time for us to withdraw and analyze what is best for ourselves and those we love. Spokespersons for the special interest groups get the publicity while ordinary people like your neighbor who mows your grass or bakes lasagna for your family when you are hospitalized is ignored.

This country was built with the "blood, sweat, and tears" of these types of people who thought of others first and themselves later. They worked and sacrificed so their children could have a better life in a country which valued freedom and morality over all else, believing that given an opportunity, most people would benefit from such a society. They fought in wars to defend the freedoms our Founding Fathers wrote in two very important documents: The Declaration of Independence and the Constitution of the

United States. However, today many people don't seem to realize that the first document says in plain English that we were given unalienable rights - life, liberty, and the pursuit of happiness - by our Creator, while the other outlines our plan of government and adds additional rights and laws to benefit all citizens. Some of these same people who don't understand these documents would question the validity of our Pledge of Allegiance mentioning a "God" and try to defend their stance by quoting the first amendment "separation of church and state," which was written in a time not far removed from a monarch dictating how the citizenry would believe. This nation, which was founded on a belief in God, is in danger of eliminating Him from public life by those who may never have even known Him.

The irony of this situation is that the very people who would be so hurt and mortified by such judicial rulings or laws often refrain from speaking out publicly about their outrage. They seem to believe that there is nothing they can do to change the course of events because, I think, they feel that their comments or feelings just don't matter. However, those who would take their religious rights away from them have no problem speaking out and spouting off to any camera or interviewer who will listen.

I fear that some of these people in the middle don't even vote in most elections, feeling that their vote wouldn't make any difference. They are unaware that, historically, one vote has made a dramatic difference in many world-wide political decisions. For example, it has been said that Adolf Hitler was placed in control of Germany's Nazi Party in 1921 by just one vote. Perhaps if he had not held that high ranking position, he would not have been elected Chancellor of that country in 1933 and over fifty million people would not have lost their lives in World War II. If that awesome thought doesn't change your mind about voting, consider that in 1960, John F. Kennedy won the Presidential election by carrying the vote in one state by less than one vote per precinct. Perhaps that one state gave him the necessary electoral votes to narrowly defeat Richard Nixon and become our 35th President.

My portion of this chapter is a bit different in concept than Deidre's and is dedicated to the hope that I can awaken in these types of people the reality of how important they really are to the democratic process of this country. I want to encourage the PIMs to let their voice be heard more often than it is now. Look in the mirror: You are an American-born or naturalized citizen with many rights guaranteed. You have the same freedom as the ACLU to speak out, peacefully meet and demonstrate for what you think is important, write your Congressmen or women, and most importantly, vote in every election. As I told Deidre (see Ch. I), voting is one of your most important rights as well as a responsibility of citizenship in this country. We are a Democratic Republic, which means the power to govern the United States of America comes from the people through their elected representatives.

The voting record of the American public is dismally low. Consider this: Even in presidential elections, almost half of the registered voters in this country don't bother to fulfill their responsibility as citizens and vote. Candidates know this and often rely on and listen to the special interest groups and those people who can be counted upon to show up at the polls and vote so they can win the election. Every vote counts today as much as it did in 1921 and 1960, as the 2000 election between George W. Bush and Al Gore demonstrated.

Several years ago, former President, Ronald Reagan, referred to you - "the people in the middle" - as the Silent Majority, and his speeches seemed to rally many who otherwise wouldn't have become involved in political campaigns and volunteer work to an activism that benefited many people, communities, and organizations. Today you can make your voice heard in your community in a variety of ways. Carefully monitor what your elected or appointed school board is doing. Consider their decisions and if you agree or disagree with their focus, let them know it. Volunteer to help in your local schools or with the parks and recreation departments in your locality. Stand for positive changes in your home town and hold your elected officials - local, state, and national - responsible for their actions.

Apathy and the "busyness" of daily life can seem to sap the strength from our country, community by community. People are so busy making a living that they count on those people whose business it is to govern to simply do their jobs. But who's "minding the store" and actually watching to ensure that things are being done as they should be? It might be that you - the parents of school-aged children, the retired grandparents, the social club member who enlists the membership in a community project, and others - are the ones who can truly make a lasting difference if only you get involved and try!

Today, more than ever, we need people who are willing to speak out against those things they believe are wrong and lead their friends and neighbors in actions to remedy problems that need fixing. All it ever takes are a few individuals who are willing to step out and lead the way. Are you willing to be such a person? If so, you can help to make positive changes for your neighborhood, your city, perhaps your state, and even your nation. More importantly, you will be a role model for your children and others around you.

Remember, you might have been placed in your little area of the world, right now, "for such a time as this!"

Two **Voices As One:** People in the middle might be here because it is their time. This is the time for them to step up and step out to make a difference that will last a lifetime and beyond. It is important for you to realize that what you accept in this life - immorality that calls itself "choice," lifestyle situations that mock a Holy and Righteous God, language and behavior that negatively impact your children - you teach to everyone around you. The choices you make affect your life and lives of those you touch because God often uses ordinary people to accomplish His extraordinary plans. Indeed we are but "Small Voices For Such A Time As This," but a small voice can transform a life or a situation just as one, small candle can illuminate a darkened room.

We encourage you to let your voice be heard!

Deidre B. Hester
Sue E. Whited

Chapter XIII - Teachers Are People Too!

"Be kind, for everyone you meet is fighting a hard battle."
- Anonymous

Voice I: A lifeline is someone who reaches out and helps you when you need it the most. Sue is one of my lifelines because during a dark period of my life, she kept me going and literally saved my teaching career. One year, when I was

179

involved in a series of car accidents and slipped into depression, Sue was there to help keep me focused. She would bring me news of how the students were doing, class sets of "Get Well Soon" cards, and posters that I could hang in my room when I returned to school. It was during this time in my life that I felt like giving up on everything, and then God would send her my way to offer me a ray of hope and one more reason to "hang in there." I remember how Larry, my husband of fourteen years, was often away from home during this time due to his Navy career. Although he was involved and very supportive, he was not there. Again, it was Sue who helped me with our two children, Shamona and Larry, Jr. Experiencing all the pain from the accidents and the pressures of being mom and dad with Larry away, it was hard for me to even think about facing one hundred or more students every day in my mental state. However, Sue was there to remind me of the many faith statements I had so often quoted to her when she found out that her youngest son, Bryan, had been diagnosed with diabetes. Now she was giving the Word back to me, and I had to accept it and move on with life, despite all its challenges. Later, after my ordeals, Sue went through several trials of her own, but the greatest had to be the loss of this son, when he went into a diabetic coma and died. I was so lost for words and how to comfort her, but I remembered how God's Word had helped me to heal and I knew it would be the only thing to help Sue as well.

Bryan was a well-built, good-looking young man with gorgeous auburn hair that would put many women to shame. I remember a statement he once made to Sue that we laughed about on several occasions. Bryan had visited the school one day to see his mom when our worst class in several years was coming back from lunch. Filled with lots of sugar and playfulness, their behavior left a lot to be desired as they entered Sue's room that day. With a smirk on his face, he remarked to his mom, "The natives are restless today!" All I could do was laugh and agree despite my embarrassment because our African-American students were really misbehaving that day. Even if I had wanted to feel angry, how could I dispute what he had said? I did wonder why Bryan had to see something like that because he was one of Sue's family members who had experienced several negative encounters with Blacks. She was trying to encourage him to look for the positives in everyone, regardless of race and then he had to see the perfect representation of negativity in those students. I told Sue I would love to have an opportunity to see Bryan personally to share and encourage him with a more positive perspective.

Fortunately before he died, we did get to share with one another several times. After his death, I was able to go on a Walk For Diabetes with Sue in his memory, and I treasure all of those memories.

Sue was in the delivery room when my youngest child was born. I remember telling her months earlier that we were "claiming" a boy. Although this term was a relatively new word for Sue, once I showed her the Scriptural basis for it, she readily grasped this concept and brought me the cutest little blue rattle with teddy bears, sailors, and boats on it. We laughed and contemplated the name

Emmanuel (God with us), then rejoiced when the doctor confirmed that the baby was a boy! From that moment on, I knew Sue and Richard would be the perfect Godparents - and they are.

Somehow through it all, we managed to survive day by day. No matter how others view us - as the answer to all the questions, the cause of all the trouble at school, or a temporary fix for a deep-rooted problem - we are still people with individual lives and many needs of our own. I have often had to tell my students when they are misbehaving, "Look, I am someone's mother, someone's wife, and loved by many - you will not treat me this way!" I go on to ask them, "Would you act like this if your mother was here? Imagine I'm your mother." These questions have been effective for many, but not for all. No, I'm not their mother, but I have had to mother students, not as a conscious effort but as the situation arises, because it is a natural reaction for me. Once when a student confided in her journal entry that she was being molested and threatened by a close relative, I comforted her with the words "God will take care of you, but you must tell." Even though I was reprimanded in writing by my principal because a police officer overheard the conversation, I knew I had done the right thing. What was in me - my Christian faith - naturally came out when it was needed. I told my principal that I would try not to mention God at school, but I couldn't promise that it wouldn't happen again. This was because even though I was a teacher in a public school, I was at heart a child of God who naturally spoke of Him. I compared it this way: "You wouldn't tell a dog that He can't bark, so don't tell me not to talk about God."

I remember my first year at Davis Middle School when I told my students to sit quietly while I went to the restroom. Those eighth graders looked at me in utter amazement and I could only respond, "Yes, I have to do that too!" They burst out in laughter as I quickly made my exit, and chuckled as I thought, "They really don't see me as a person."

Teachers wear many hats and I am a person with many roles. I am a woman, God's minister, a wife, a mother, a daughter, a sister, a teacher, a colleague, a friend, and an acquaintance. To view me as only a teacher is to miss so many other valuable parts because I am a person, just like you.

Voice II: Every day untold numbers of people leave home in the morning and drive, walk, or car pool to work. Many of them carry their lunches, a bag full of paperwork, pens, books, and perhaps a laptop computer with them as they enter a building, find their key, and open a door which leads to another world. This world contains many seats, a few tables, a variety of supplies, a chalk or dry erase board, and a bulletin board. These people are teachers and within their classroom, they affect their little corner of the world in many ways. However, most of their students have never thought or don't even care that the person whose name is above the door of that room, is a person with the same needs, wants, and dreams as everyone else in their domain. Rarely does the thought come to the minds of some administrators, parents, and students that "teachers are people too!"

Every day teachers go to work, leaving behind challenges, struggles, heartache, and who knows what else to greet other people's children and attempt to teach them something new. Daily, all kinds of paperwork needs to be completed, lesson plans designed, phone calls made or returned, classrooms of students managed, and curriculum taught with enthusiasm and energy. Deep within, their hearts may be breaking over a failed marriage, a wayward child, a court decision, upcoming surgery for themselves or a loved one, the military deployment of a spouse, the possibility of nursing home care for a parent, or a myriad of other issues that threaten to topple their sanity. But all anyone ever sees is Mr. Austin or Mrs. Bell unlocking that door, beginning another day, and trying to put a smile on his/her face. Our public needs to know and understand that we were people before we became teachers and people we remain.

One of the most amusing aspects of this job is meeting students as you go about your daily life after school or on the weekends. Shortly after I began my teaching career in middle school, I was shopping for groceries at a nearby store, and encountered one of my students and her parent in one of the aisles. You would have thought the child, who was accustomed to seeing me teach her history or reading, would faint from shock at seeing me in a "regular" part of the world, outside the walls of the school. Of all things, I was dressed in jeans and a sweatshirt! This situation has multiplied itself many times and I never cease to be amused as the reaction of students when they see me in the "real" world. Most are pleased and want to introduce me to a parent or sibling, but some seem to have never thought that I'm a person just like them who needs food, gasoline, or maybe some Tylenol!

I have worked with many teachers who have gone through difficult, challenging days while attempting to continue to teach the students who are under their care and supervision. While I tried to remain sympathetic, supportive, and compassionate, I never truly understood what they were going through until a two to three period when I felt like the Biblical character, Job, as one challenging situation after another befell me. During this time, I lived through unbelievable problems with my grown children over which I had absolutely no control and the untimely death of my youngest son at age 28 from diabetic complications. Then a lump appeared on my neck that needed two needle biopsies for a (blessed) benign diagnosis, and uterine fibroids plagued me for months before ultimately beginning to hemorrhage while I was trying to teach my last class one October day. When this problem required major surgery, I did what I had done during the entire challenging period, and held fast to the promise that God would not give me more than He and I could handle together. I continued to teach my students, unlocking that door every morning except for the twenty-one days plus Christmas vacation when I was absent for surgical leave. I dealt with my problems when I had to, but welcomed the diversion of teaching 128 students during the day to momentarily take my mind away from the heart-breaking drama that was happening with my family and within my body. I was definitely a teacher, but so much more a person with all the troubles I was struggling to overcome.

Teachers are like everyone else - the cashier at the grocery store, the mechanic at the car dealership, or your beautician down the road - living through the good times and the bad, just doing the best they can. Their daily job description might be different because they interact with children and specific curriculum every day instead of money, spark plugs, or curling irons, but they have families that need them, sick children at home, or a spouse with problems that interfere with their ability to focus solely on the problems individual students have within their classes. Your child is an important part of their life this year, but because this teacher - this person - has wants and needs of his/her own, individual students cannot be the only focus of his/her life.

So the next time you walk into your neighborhood school for a parent-teacher conference or when you feel the need to pick up the phone and call your child's teacher, please remember that the individual speaking to you is a person who may be facing challenging situations in their own life. He/she should be willing to meet you more than halfway in working with your student, but they don't need personal attacks, impatience, or preconceived notions of incompetence or worse still, prejudice. Work with them to help your child, and always remember that just like you, "teachers are people too."

Two **Voices As One:** An old Indian story ends with the proverb that "to understand another, you must walk a mile in his moccasins." That advice could apply to this chapter because we have tried to describe the daily walk that teachers take during their careers. Both of us agree that many people fail to see teachers as the people they are. We are professionals who have so many daily and long-term responsibilities that it almost seems unfair for life to throw illness, family problems, and additional challenges our way. However it happens all the time to many educators, and when it does, teachers do the best they know how to do in what may be very difficult circumstances. While they have chosen a career in which they work with children or young people, adults, computers, deadlines, and curriculum, they also have to fulfill the other roles that life has handed them - those of wife/husband, mother/father, child, sibling, church member, and neighbor, among others. Please remember that most days their plate is very full. However, many teachers try to remain positive and upbeat while teaching yet another concept to another class filled with your children. We are people, with all the frailties you may see when you look in the mirror, but not everyone realizes that. Now you do!

Deidre B. Hester
Sue E. Whited

Chapter XIV - Just For You: A God-Shaped Void

"Faith is a gift, but you <u>can</u> ask for it."

- Fulton Oursler

Voice II: I was thinking about this book early one morning when the shower spray was helping me to awaken and shampoo was rinsing down over my forehead. Suddenly, it was as if I received a spiritual message from above, giving me the topic for a concluding chapter. The title, "Just For You: A God-Shaped Void" came to me as I remembered a years old experience that had faded from my memory. I was walking down the hall of my school when a lovely, young teacher from upstairs came up to me. Out of the blue, she told me that she was searching for meaning in life, and knew I was a Christian. She said that she wanted to know if there was any way I could help her. I remember smiling at her and thinking, "What can I say? God, please don't fail me now!" However, what came out of my mouth was profound and perfect, definitely God sent. I told her that the reason she was searching was because her Heavenly Father had created her with a God-shaped void that only He could fill. No matter what she tried instead of Him, she would still be empty and unfulfilled. He was waiting for her to turn to Him. Her face lit up immediately and she absolutely gushed at me, "That's it - that's perfect! I have been searching everywhere, trying different religions, meditation, yoga - you name it. I always end up feeling more lonely than ever because nothing ever works." I gave her a hug and later that week brought her a modern translation of the Bible that she and her roommate began reading. At the end of that school year, she moved to a distant state and I don't know what happened to her or her search. But I do remember the warm, peaceful feeling I experienced as she walked away when I realized that I had been placed in that hall perhaps for the very reason that God needed a messenger to draw a lost child to Him. He gave me that description that so aptly fit her need.

It is only fitting that we end our book with a chapter that gives hope and encouragement to those who read it. Since Deidre and I are both Christians and not only draw our strength from each other, but also from our relationship with God, we could not neglect sharing Him with you in a personal way as our book draws to a close. I think God wants you to know just how much He loves you, so He gave me the idea to add this last chapter "just for you."

In my career as a teacher, I have met many people who are in the same situation as that young lady. It's easy to recognize that young people are searching because they have yet to define their identity. However, many adults are just as lost and seem to be looking for meaning to their lives also. No matter how high or low the salary, whether they live in a five-bedroom home or a one-bedroom apartment, drive a BMW or a rusted-out Chevy, adults in this country and around the world are continually searching for the answer to the question, "Why am I here?" An analogy might be the driving, homing instinct that causes salmon to swim against currents, around dams, and incredibly - up waterfalls - as they struggle to reach their ancestral spawning grounds to lay eggs. Humans also have a homing instinct, sixteenth century Protestant theologian, John Calvin thought when he wrote these words:

"There exists in the human mind, and indeed, by natural instinct, a sense of the Deity."

Augustine, one of the greatest theologians of Western Christianity, speaking of his and other's relationships with God said:

"Hearts are restless until they find
their rest (ease) in You."

Current devotional writer, David Roper,
continues with the thought,

"We are born and we live for the
express purpose of knowing and
loving God. He is the source of
our life, and our hearts are restless
until they come to Him."

Some world religions teach that it takes
many levels of consciousness and several
lifetimes to perfect life and reach the ultimate
goal. Other belief systems tell people to do
the best they can for their fellow man, live life
to the fullest, and they will be happy. But look
into the eyes of the people you see on the
street, in the mall, at the gym, or the bank and
you will probably see expressions of sadness,
desperation, futility, and emptiness. If these
people could only learn that their Creator
knows and loves them, what a difference that
could make in their lives. It is such an

awesome thought to realize that the God of the universe is waiting for a one-on-one relationship with each of us. He will not force His way into our lives, but will patiently wait until He is invited.

I would like to encourage each of you to give His Word, the Bible, a chance to explain how you can have the relationship God desires to have with each of you and why it is necessary. In this Book you will find that:

- God loves you and has a great plan for your life. In Genesis 1:27 the Bible says that God created you in His image to have a relationship with Him.

- He wants you to experience a full and wonderful life. In John 10:10, Jesus says that He came to give you "abundant life."

- Something got in the way of our relationship with God. That something is sin. Romans 3:23 says that everyone has "sinned and fallen short of the glory of God." This means that we all have failed to meet God's standard for how we ought to live. We will never live up to His standards because God is holy and we are not.

- Sin separates us from God and sin always requires punishment. Romans 6:23 states that the "wages of sin is death," which means eternal separation from God. This scripture doesn't leave us hanging there, though, but continues with these words: "but the gift of God is eternal life through Jesus Christ, our Lord."

- God has made a way for us to be forgiven for our sins, and that way was through His Son. Romans 5:8 tells us "But God demonstrated his love for us in this, that while we were still sinners, Christ died for us."

- God will accept Jesus' death on the cross as payment for our sins.

- Jesus' resurrection from the dead on that first Easter provides our assurance of eternal life through a belief in Him. Jesus himself said in John 14:6 that "I am the Way, the Truth, and the Life. No one comes to the Father, but through Me."

The choice is up to you. Are you willing to stop living your life without Jesus, turn from your sins, and welcome Him into your heart? Romans 10:9 tells you that

> "If you confess with your mouth
> 'Jesus is Lord' and believe in your
> heart that God raised Him from
> the dead, you will be saved."

Saved from the power of sin! Saved from eternal separation from God in Hell! Saved to live a new life! The Apostle John, the disciple of Jesus said,

> "To all who received Him, to
> those who believed in His name,
> He gave the right to become
> children of God." (John 1:12)

The gift of salvation is just that - a gift from your Heavenly Father (Ephesians 2:8) because if a person could earn it by being good enough, then it wouldn't be free - but it is. How incredibly wonderful is that!

I hope you decide to fill your God-shaped void today with the loving relationship your Heavenly Father wants to give you. Many people will downplay this gospel presentation with a snicker and a laugh, telling you that I am just one of those crazy "right-wing Christians." However, did they ever stop to think that I just may be right? What if I am? You have everything to gain and nothing to lose by checking out that Book - the Bible. Read it for yourself; maybe starting with the book that the Rev. Billy Graham recommends for new believers - the Gospel of John which you can find in the New Testament.

Life today can sometimes be overwhelming. Why go through it alone? Invite Jesus, the Son of God, into your life today and He will be with you now and forever.

Voice I: In our book's last chapter, I want to conclude with this thought: I believe that one of the greatest errors the Christian community has ever made was to allow God to inadvertently be taken out of our public and some of our private school systems. Like a wobbly house of cards or a line of dominos destined to fall, the effect of this action has led America to begin removing all reference to religion or God in public life. Proof of this can be seen in the current lawsuit to remove the phrase "One Nation Under God" from the Pledge of Allegiance, or the actual removal of the Ten Commandments monument from an Alabama courthouse in the summer of 2003. Most recently, I saw news reports about a man who was charged with damaging property in a public library. He destroyed a magazine cover depicting intimate kissing between homosexual men, stating that he felt such a cover was offensive and a detriment to any children who might see it. Instead of choosing to protect its youngest customers, the library is considering legal action against this man, stating that a public library is just that - public, and the magazine should be there for those who want to read it.

Many of our forefathers and early
settlers who came to this country were God-
believing men and women. Their beliefs
became the cornerstone and founding
principles upon which some of our country's
most precious documents were written. The
Pilgrims came here for freedom to worship, as
did the Quakers who wanted variety in their
ways of worship. However both groups just
wished to honor and serve the One, True,
Living God. So how is it that a God-based
and God-founded country has become so
universally accepting that we now allow
satanic images, humanistic teachings, and
ungodly principles to rule in some of our
churches and schools under the
misrepresentation of the first amendment's
Freedom of Religion? This amendment gave
us the right to worship God as we pleased
without the controlling interference of the
government. Somehow we have allowed this
"separation of church and state" to diminish
our voices as Christians and lessen our
courage to speak out boldly against these anti-
Godly teachings and immoral practices or
ideals. Since this country professes to be

predominately Christian, the Christian voice should be the one most heard, but it isn't. Every other group tends to influence what we see, hear, and think more than it should. We have shown a lack of unity and example as a God-based nation. It is vital that we return to the truth that God established America and this young country will not succeed without Him as the basis for how we live our lives.

We are living in a time when abominations unto God are being popularized by television shows and laughed at without any regards to God's Word. The institution of marriage is also becoming a mockery, being damaged beyond repair through the legalization of same-sex unions, and the easy availability of divorce, because we are not choosing to speak out and protect it. We need to wake up and take America back for God. Phrases like "One Nation Under God," "God Bless America," and "In God We Trust" were not merely statements of chance. They were God-inspired and God-ordained statements of faith given to those men who would begin a proud nation known as these United States of America.

Some of us as Christians are failing to be a prevailing light to a lost and dying world. We are a nation with such a wide void because we have not put God in His proper place at the head of our lives. We are suffering with a chasm so deep that only God and His Word can fill in the empty spaces. When God created us, he blew a breath of life - a part of Himself - into each of us, so we all share God's DNA, His Spirit. How awesome that an omniscient, all-knowing God could look through the tunnel of time and place a God-shaped desire in each of us in order that mankind could have a relationship and fellowship with Him, and be redeemed back to Him. Sin does separate us, but we can be reunited through Jesus Christ. He did this and also gave us the choice to come to Him freely.

Only God can fill the "voids" in our lives because He is the missing piece to the puzzle, the answer to the riddle, and the fulfillment to our individual searches throughout life. We will never be satisfied until we get back to our Father. I am always amazed when adopted children are placed in some of the best homes, yet grow up with an emptiness so prevalent that they feel the need to search for their "real" parents - the source of their origin. Television talk show host, Montel Williams, has often featured segments with siblings and parents being reunited after years of separation. So often these people are able to determine who their true family members are long before it is even revealed. This is because likenesses attract us. It is an instinct of knowing that we belong; there is something in us that recognizes familiarity. Some siblings have the same daddy or the same mom and dad. Likewise, Christians share the same Daddy regardless of race, culture, or denominational differences.

We are all given an opportunity to come back to God, our Creator, and our place of true origin. We can be called the "Sons (Daughters) of God" through the example of our Big Brother, Jesus Christ, whereby we may call out to God, "Abba Father," ("Papa God") and be born again into the Family of God (Galatians 4: 3-7 and Romans 8:15-17).

Imagine yourself as a Child of God, crawling up into the lap of the One who has all the answers and waits to give you the love you've longed for all your life. He is waiting to supply all your needs and welcome you home. God is our Father - our true Parent.

The decision is solely ours. We must choose good over evil, right over wrong, and God's teaching over man's logic and intelligence. The belief in God and His Word is what built America and that is what will sustain us. Righteous living is never easy. When you stand for God's teachings, people sometimes label you a "religious fanatic." Matthew 5:11 quotes Jesus as saying,

> "Blessed are you when people
> insult you, persecute you, and
> falsely say all kinds of evil against
> you because of Me."

Matthew 7:13-14 reminds us that it is far easier to go the world's way rather than God's way. It reminds me of a poem Robert Frost concluded with these words:

> "I took the road less traveled, and
> that has made all the difference."

I have come to realize that I have also chosen the less traveled road, God's road. Traveling with Him as He leads has made an important difference in my life which will last into eternity.

Two **Voices As One:** We would rather stand for God and remain "Small Voices" than to compromise to please man and become well-known ones. The peace that comes from knowing and trusting Him is worth everything. Stop searching for that kind of peace from anything the world may offer. No job, wealth, mate, or goal will ever fulfill what God has already purposed for your life. You can't buy it, but if you seek true meaning for your life, you will find it in God. (Matthew 7:7-8)

"Those who cling to worthless idols
forfeit the grace that could be theirs…
…Salvation comes from the Lord."
- Jonah 2: 8-9

For Such A Time As This...
...We Are But Small Voices

Deidre B. Hester
Sue E. Whited

The Two Small Voices

Voice I - Then

Voice I – Now

Voice II – Then

Voice II – Now

Two Voices As One

About the Authors

Voice I: Deidre B. Hester and her husband, Larry, are both ministers with True Gospel Ministries Evangelical House of God located in Suffolk, VA. They have two children, Shamona and Larry, Jr. Mrs. Hester has been an educator for over fifteen years and has taught in both public and private Christian schools. She has also worked with Alternative education, including special programs for delinquent youth. She proudly, but temporarily resides in her family's native hometown of Gates County, NC, where she teaches English to eighth grade students at Central Middle School. In the summer of 2004, Mrs. Hester and her children will join her husband in Japan where he is currently stationed aboard the USS Kitty Hawk in Yokosuka, Japan.

Voice II: Sue E. Whited and her husband, Richard, are both teachers with Hampton City Schools in Hampton, VA., and are the parents of two sons, Ric, also of Hampton and Bryan, deceased. Obtaining college credits in several states during husband's tour of duty with the U.S. Air Force, Mrs. Whited graduated from Christopher Newport College in Newport News, VA., and has taught sixth and eighth grade students the subjects of reading and social studies for almost twenty years. She and her husband attend Liberty Baptist Church in Hampton, where she enjoys participating in the music ministry and both serve as workers in the preschool nursery program.

Acknowledgements

We wish to thank the many people who have supported us and our "Voices" in this endeavor:

Voice I

- To my most endearing and dependable friend, Sue Whited, who made this book possible by writing, compiling, typing, and editing it several times!! Sue, it was my dream, but you surely helped to make it happen.
- I am so grateful for the love, help, and support from my wonderful husband, Larry D. Hester, Sr., and my children, Shamona and Larry, Jr. They have shown patience with me every step of the way and continued to motivate me by expecting a written, revised, and completed book.
- In loving memory, I wish to thank my maternal grandmother, Mrs. Lessie Mae

Shambley, who always set a Godly example for me.

- I wish to earnestly thank my pastor and oldest brother, Bishop Daniel W. Boone, Sr. and his wife, Therferm. He has given me great teaching and advice that has helped me my entire life, and his wife has been a life-long encourager to me as well.
- A special thanks to my beautiful mother, Mrs. Carrie Boone, my other siblings and family members, including my husband's mother, Mrs. Ida Mae Hester and her family. I wish to also thank my loving church family who have supported me in so many ways.
- Another special thank you to Mr. Richard Whited for his special title page design, because it truly represents our book; and to Mrs. Sue Edwards and Mrs. Trina Jones for taking the time to proof our book, to Pernessa Seele, and Mr. and Mrs. Spurgion Benning for reading, editing, or listening to our book, in parts or whole.

- And last, but in reality first, I give thanks to God who makes all things possible.

Voice II

- My eternal gratitude to Deidre, my lifeline and friend, who has impacted my life in so many positive ways.

- For always being there for me through their prayers and support, I want to thank my parents, A. Paul Saunders (dec.) and Gretta Saunders. I am thankful that I grew up in a home where God was a part of my life for as long as I can remember.

- A loving "thank you" to my husband, Richard, for putting up with all the work and frustration from this "budding" author. Your original page design is awesome!

- My endless thanks to Sue Edwards - administrator, teacher, colleague, and friend - for many reasons, but specifically for proofing our book and encouraging our efforts.

- My gratitude to Mary Anne Gaus for her availability and invaluable technical computer advice and help.
- My appreciation to Dr. Daniel Forshee for his ministerial wisdom and insight in helping to proof Ch. XIV.
- My thanks to HCS (you know who you are) for the iMac laptop which enabled me to write and edit in many locations.

Two Voices As One

The "Two Voices" together wish to thank:

- Mrs. Gretta Saunders for all she has done in helping us to publish this book, and Mrs. Sue Edwards for being such an encourager to us both.
- To our many other family members, friends, and colleagues who encouraged us to continue with our "labor of love" - this book - we thank you.

- Our thanks to Heartland Samplers, Inc for some of the quotations used in this publication, and to the Winans for the pertinent lyrics from their song, "Bring Back the Days of 'Yay and Nay'"
- Our thanks to David L. Hancock with Morgan James Publishing for all his patience and dedication in helping us to publish our work.
- Since we dedicated this book to God, we want to thank Him for bringing the 'two voices' together in the first place. We had no idea what our friendship would mean to us or others, but we have learned to trust Him and follow where He leads.

Epilogue: Words of Wisdom for our readers:

"We make a living by what we get, but we make a life by what we give."
                                    - Arthur Ashe

In the end, each of us will be judged not by our standard of living, but by our measure of giving; not by our measure of wealth, but by our simple goodness.
                                    - Anonymous

Unexpected kindness is the most powerful, least costly and most underrated agent of human change. Kindness that catches us by surprise brings out the best in our natures.
                                    - Anonymous

"I will permit no man to narrow or degrade my soul by making me hate him."
- Booker T. Washington

Prejudice distorts what it sees, deceives when it speaks, and destroys when it acts.
- Anonymous

Life is like a buffet line: there are no waiters, so you have to serve yourself!
- Anonymous

There is no right way to do the wrong thing.
- Anonymous

"If you live for the next world, you get this one in the deal; but if you live only for this world, you lose them both."
- C. S. Lewis

We always have time for the things we put first.
- Anonymous

"To get out of a difficulty, one usually must go through it."
- Samuel Easton

Laughter is a tranquilizer with no side effects.
- Anonymous

"The man who does not read good books has no advantage over the man who can't read."
- Mark Twain

"I am sorry for the people who do not read the Bible every day. I wonder why they deprive themselves of the strength and of the pleasure."
- Woodrow Wilson

"We can do no great things, only small things with great love."
- Mother Teresa

"It is not how much we have but how much we enjoy, that makes happiness."
- C. H. Spurgeon

"I thank God for my handicaps, for, through them, I have found myself, my work, and my God."
                              - Helen Keller

Happiness is not the absence of conflict, but the ability to deal with it.
                              - Anonymous

Every person in this world is a dream of God.
                              - Anonymous

A good exercise for the heart is to bend down and help another up.
                              - Anonymous

A good traffic rule on the Road of Life: When you meet temptation, keep to the right.
                              - Anonymous

Although salvation is a free gift, we sometimes forget that we still must ask for it.
                              - Anonymous

"Wherever a person turns he can find someone who needs him. Even if it is a little thing - do something for which there is no pay - but the privilege of just doing it. Remember, you don't live in this world all on your own."

     - Albert Schweitzer

"No one can make you feel inferior without your consent."

     - Eleanor Roosevelt

"I have lived a long time, and the longer I live, the more convincing proofs I see of this truth - that God governs in the affairs of men."

     - Benjamin Franklin

The butterfly counts not months but moments and yet has time enough.

     - Anonymous

"It is never too late to give up our prejudices."

     - Thoreau

Friendship is a cozy shelter from life's rainy days.

     - Anonymous

"I don't think much of a man who is not wiser today than he was yesterday."

> \- Abraham Lincoln

Let the words I speak today be soft and tender, for tomorrow I may have to eat them!

> \- Anonymous

"The secret of my success? It is simple and is found in the Bible: 'In all thy ways acknowledge Him and He shall direct thy paths.'"

> \- George Washington Carver

"All I have seen teaches me to trust the Creator for all I have not seen."

> \- Ralph Waldo Emerson

"God made you as you are in order to use you as He planned."

> \- S. C. McAuley

Worry is wasting today's time to clutter up tomorrow's opportunities with yesterday's troubles.

> \- Anonymous

Good friends are like stars. You can't always see them, but you know they're always there.
- Anonymous

"The only real progress is spiritual progress."
- Patsy Love Miller

"There is a part of us that only God can touch."
- Bishop Daniel Boone

To experience a rainbow you have to make it through the rain.
- Anonymous

"Look hard enough and you will always find a light."
- Rachael Joy Scott

"In spite of everything, I still believe that people are really good at heart."
- Anne Frank

"What will we leave behind… Are we too blind to see… How can we close our eyes… What will our legacy be?"

> \- Bryan M. Whited
> 1970 – 1999

"God gave me the gift of teaching to teach the total child, and that is what I do. I teach the total child"

> \- Deidre Hester

"A smile and a kind word never costs us anything."

> \- Sam Boone
> (Deidre's Great Grandfather)

Deidre B. Hester
Sue E. Whited